FLORISTS' REVIEW

one-hundred-and-one

101

WEDDING

BOUQUETS

PUBLISHER: Frances Dudley

EXECUTIVE EDITOR: Talmage McLaurin

AUTHOR AND EDITOR: Shelley Urban

PHOTOGRAPHER: Stephen Smith

SPONSOR: California Cut Flower Commission

FLORAL DESIGN: Ty Leslie, AIFD
                      Talmage McLaurin, AIFD
                      René van Rems, AIFD, PFCI

*Florists' Review's 101 Wedding Bouquets with
How-To Instructions* was designed and produced
by Florists' Review Enterprises, Inc.;
3641 SW Plass; Topeka, Kansas 66611-2588

Printed in the United States by The John Henry
Company, Lansing, Michigan.

Design and Typesetting by Artemis,
Topeka, Kansas.

ISBN: 0-9714860-0-X

FLORISTS' REVIEW

101

one-hundred-and-one

WEDDING
BOUQUETS

contents

baskets 6

collar techniques 14

composites 22

cones 30

contemporary cascades 38

fans 46

foliage techniques 54

garden 62

garden cascades 70

geometrics 78

handle treatments 86

hand-tied 94

jeweled 102

monobotanicals 110

nosegays 118

pomanders 126

purses 134

scepters 142

sheaves 150

support structures 158

tussie-mussies 166

veiled 174

Victorian 182

wrapped 190

wreaths 198

grand finale 206

bird's nest

1 Remove the handle from a straight-handled bouquet holder. Saturate it and glue it into the center of the bird's nest.

This nature-made basket is blooming with springtime florals.

Attached to a large, flower-filled bird's nest, a permanent wired-vine handle transforms the pretty arrangement into a nature-made spring basket for flower girls and attendants. Fresh ivy, artfully entwined around the faux vine handle, is the ideal accessory.

A bounty of pastel-hued spring florals, including *Ranunculuses*, hyacinths, and lisianthuses, are tucked into the bird's nest basket. This beautifully finished presentation—a spring icon transformed into a charming wedding accessory—is absolutely fabulous for any wedding scheduled during this delightful season, especially if held outdoors.

2 Attach artificial wired vines to each side of the bird's nest. Entwine the vines at the top to complete the handle.

3 Arrange the flowers in the foam. Insert fresh ivy into the foam, and weave it onto and around the handle.

materials:

Ranunculuses
hyacinths
lisianthuses
ivy
premade bird's nest
artificial wired vines
Wedding Belle Bouquet Holder
hot glue

garden grown

A flower-covered basket fresh from the garden.

1 Cover the basket's handle with fern. Secure the fern to the handle with a wrapping of barked wire.

2 Using floral adhesive, glue stock florets to the outside of the basket. Cover the entire outer surface.

3 Fill up the basket with stock florets, or glue a stock-covered cardboard lid over the basket's opening. Finish with a wrapping of ribbon and bows.

With a fresh-from-the-garden appearance, this lavish basket, featuring a covering of stock florets and a fern-wrapped handle, conveys the charm of a warm summer day. It may be used for both indoor and outdoor ceremonies and suits bridesmaids as well as flower girls.

Once it is covered with a full, lush fern such as foxtail (*Asparagus meyeri*) or star asparagus (*A. deflexis*), the handle is wrapped with barked wire, resulting in a garden-grown effect. Then, the stock florets are glued to the basket with floral adhesive. To keep the pretty blooms looking fresh, a mist of antitranspirant is recommended.

materials:
stock florets
foxtail fern (*Asparagus meyeri*) or
    star asparagus (*Asparagus deflexis*)
handled basket
barked wire
Oasis Floral Adhesive

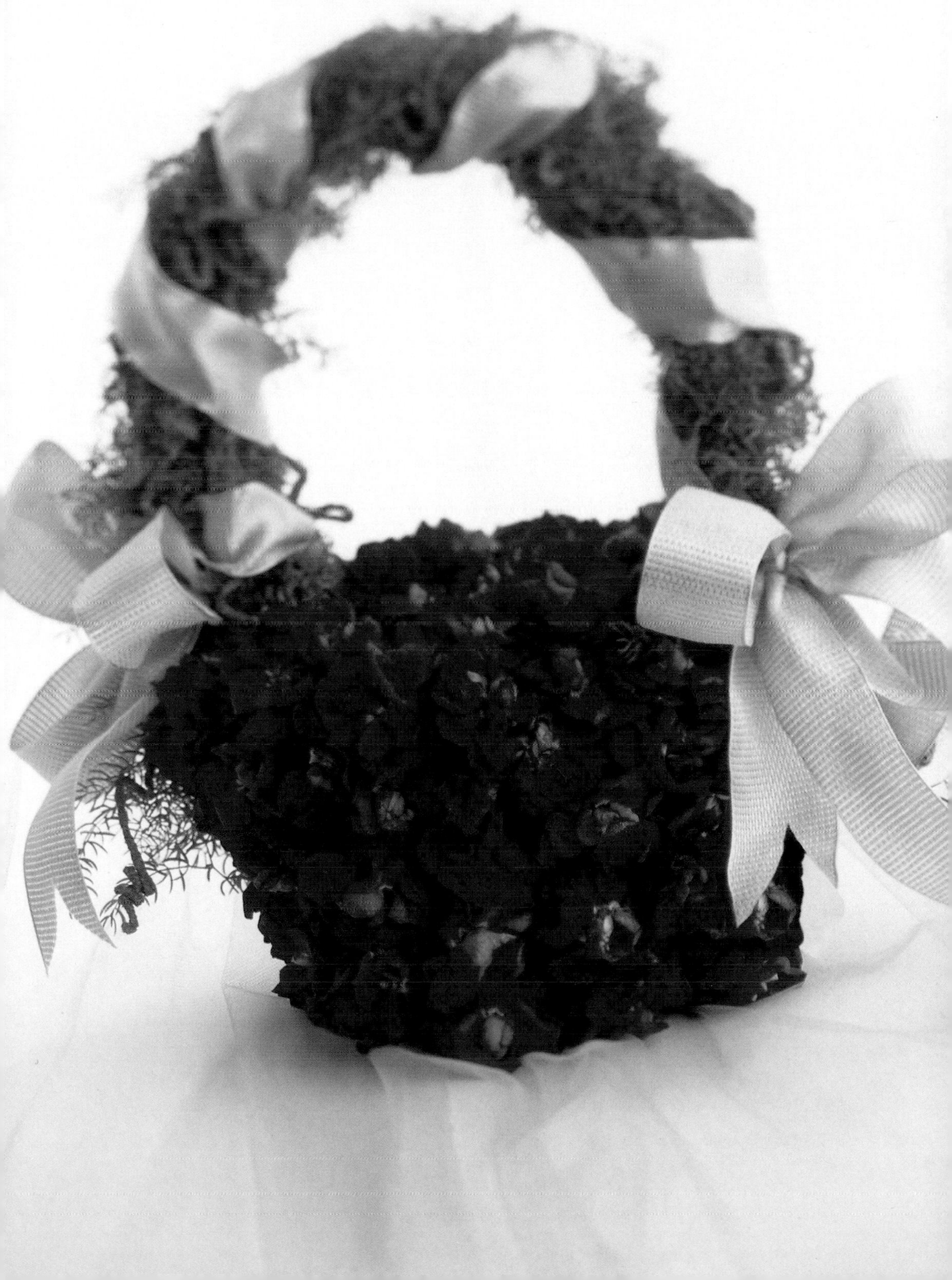

bountiful basket

1 Remove the handle from a basket. Attach a square handle made from artificial wired vines.

2 Remove the handle from a bouquet holder, and glue it inside the plastic-lined basket.

3 Adorn the vines with foliage materials such as the blue lepto. Wrap raffia at the grasping point to finish the handle.

A harvest-inspired selection overflowing with autumn's bounty.

Laden with the fruits of fall, this abundantly filled basket bouquet, composed of several types of berries, cottage yarrow, *Sedum*, *Banksia*, *Leucadendron*, *Hydrangeas*, and more, is almost overflowing with autumn's bounty. A large bouquet holder, from which the handle has been removed, is placed inside the lined basket. The florals are arranged in the bouquet holder, which helps achieve a lavishly full look with a modest amount of materials.

An artificial vine handle, treated with fresh *Leptospermum* and a raffia wrap, adds to the harvest-inspired presentation.

materials:

Banksia
Leucadendron
Camellia foliage
millet (*Setaria*)
cottage yarrow
Sedum
Hydrangeas
blue lepto (*Leptospermum*)
persimmons
Pyracantha berries
Wedding Belle Bouquet Holder
plastic liner
artificial wired vines

holiday glitz

Gloriously gilded, this simple basket is ready for winter nuptials

1 Spray an inexpensive handled basket with metallic gold paint.

2 Hot-glue a saturated foam cage inside the basket. Arrange carnations in the cage.

3 Remove the foliage from the seeded *Eucalyptus*, and paint the seeds gold. Once the paint has dried, place the gilded *Eucalyptus* into the design.

Painted gold and accented with a Gucci-striped ribbon, an inexpensive woven basket, filled with miniature carnations, is decorated for the holidays. The fresh-cut blooms are accessorized by seeded *Eucalyptus*, which has also been gilded in grand holiday fashion. Although naturally long-lasting, the miniature carnations are arranged in a saturated foam cage, so the arrangement can be made in advance and still look fresh on the wedding day.

For winter weddings, particularly those scheduled during the yuletide season, this simple basket bouquet is affordable yet elegant and could serve beautifully for flower girls and bridesmaids.

materials:

miniature carnations
seeded *Eucalyptus*
woven basket
ribbon
Brilliant Gold spray paint
Aquafoam cage
hot glue

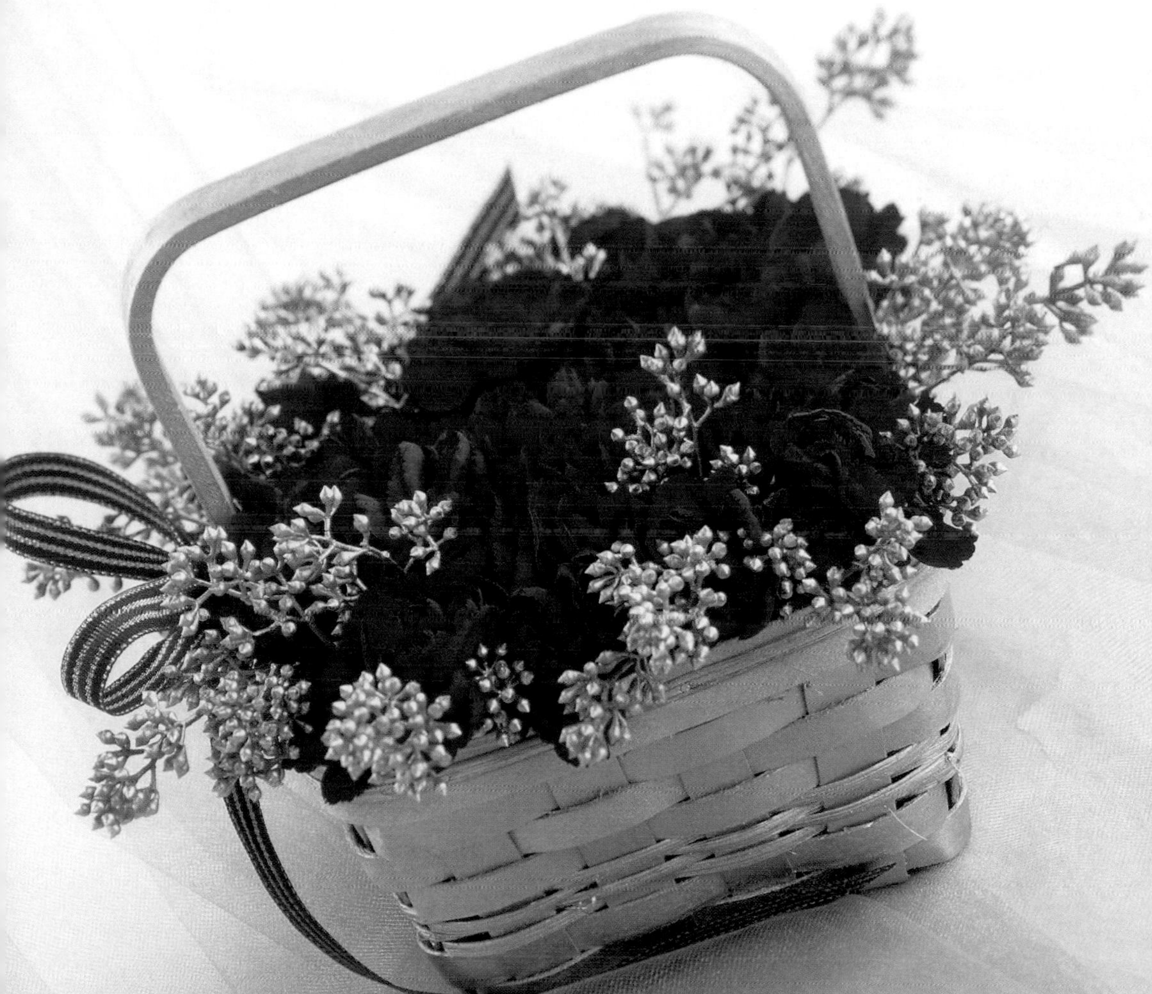

willow wrap

Curly willow lends a woodsy effect to an all-rose arrangement.

This beautiful composition of 'Akito' hybrid tea roses and 'Cream Gracia' spray roses, ranging from buds to blooms to petal-dropped calyxes, is enhanced with a vining collar of curly willow, which adds movement and dimension, not to mention a woodsy effect, to the monochromatic creation.

The curly willow, which is adorned with a twining of pearled cording, is secured to the bouquet holder with pins made from heavy-gauge wire. Although the pearled cording softens the rough-hewn collar, the bouquet has an outdoorsy feel and would be perfect for *al fresco* springtime events.

1 Piece together a collar of curly willow using wire that has been covered with brown floral tape. Permanent wired vine may also be used.

2 Decorate the curly willow collar with pearled cording, entwined among the vines.

3 Create four hairpins from heavy-gauge wire. Use these to pin the willow collar into the bouquet holder.

materials:

'Akito' standard roses
'Cream Gracia' spray roses
curly willow
Wedding Belle Bouquet Holder
pearled cording
heavy-gauge wire

protea petals

1 Cut off the outer petals of a 'Pink Ice' *Protea*. Divide the petals into individual pieces that can be placed separately.

2 Staple the petals around the perimeter of a cardboard ribbon flange to make the collar. Slip the petal-covered flange over the bouquet holder's handle.

3 Arrange flowers in the bouquet holder. Tape *Protea* petals to chenille stems, and add them to the arrangement.

Hot summer hues reside in this vibrant gathering of bicolor 'La Minuet' spray roses, *Epidendrum* orchids, and sprays of permanent berries. The feathery, collared effect is achieved with individual 'Pink Ice' *Protea* petals that have been attached to a cardboard ribbon flange. More *Protea* petals, taped to chenille stems, are arranged amid the flowers.

The eye-catching creation, with its summery range of colors and textures, seems best suited for formal occasions, but the coordinating yellow ribbon streamers hint at more casual applications.

materials:

'La Minuet' spray roses
Epidendrum orchids
'Pink Ice' *Protea*
permanent berry sprays
Wedding Belle Bouquet Holder
chenille stems
floral tape

Celosia ring

Garden annuals form a natural collar for fall weddings.

1 Cluster several stems of *Celosia*, and bind them with waterproof tape. Nestle a bouquet holder into the *Celosia* cluster.

2 Arrange flowers in the bouquet holder. Attach chinaberries to wired picks, and place them into the design.

3 Wrap bearded wheat with copper beading wire. Add the wheat in swirls around the bouquet's edge. Wrap *Celosia* stems with peach ribbon, and cover the ribbon with a layer of beading wire.

Luscious peach roses and fresh green chinaberries are arranged in a bouquet holder that is nestled into an impressive grouping of lime green *Celosia* (cockscomb), which forms a natural textured collar. The *Celosia* stems are tightly wrapped with peach ribbon and are further adorned with a haphazard treatment of copper beading wire. The ribbon wrap conceals the *Celosia* stems and helps secure the bouquet holder amid the fluffy green blossoms.

Attached to wired picks, fresh bearded wheat is tightly wrapped with copper beading wire and placed, in swirls, around the bouquet's edge.

materials:
roses
chinaberries
Celosia (cockscomb)
bearded wheat
peach ribbon
copper beading wire
Wedding Belle Bouquet Holder
wired picks
Oasis waterproof tape

8 pearls and lace

Premium flowers are trimmed with elegant accessories.

1 Staple the end of a satin ribbon to a flange. Looping the ribbon through the opening, begin wrapping the flange. When the flange is completely covered, staple the ribbon in place.

2 Glue the ribbon-wrapped flange to the base of the bouquet holder.

Dripping with pearls and accented with lace, this gorgeous orchid bouquet is designed for formal wedding ceremonies. The collar, a ribbon-wrapped cardboard flange accessorized with pearl strands and sprays, as well as bows and ribbon streamers, is glued to the base of a bouquet holder. The holder's handle is further adorned by a premade, pearl-and-lace-encrusted cover.

The *pièce de résistance*, a pristine collection of white *Phalaenopsis* orchids, is arranged in a mounded formation, and the collar's pearl and ribbon accessories are interspersed among the pretty, moth-like petals.

3 Attach trim—bows, ribbons, and pearls—to wood picks. Insert picks into foam. Use hot glue to secure the handle cover. Arrange orchids.

materials:

Phalaenopsis orchids
ribbon and pearl trimmings
satin ribbon
cardboard ribbon flange
Wedding Belle Bouquet Holder
premade bouquet handle cover
wood picks
hot glue
stapler and staples

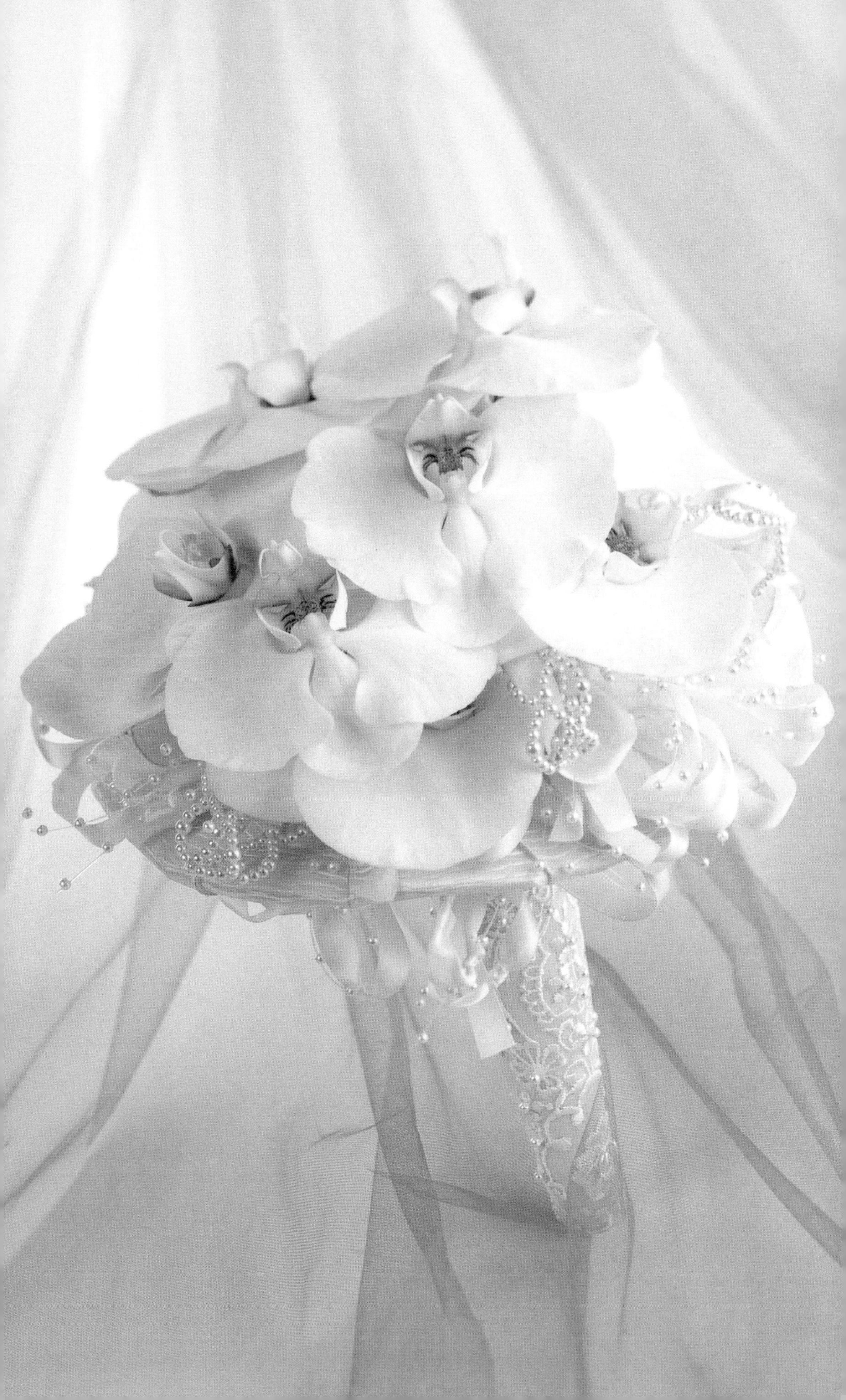

glamellia

1 Slice open *Gladiolus* florets, and remove pistils and stamens. Nestle florets in groups around a single *Gladiolus* bud. Insert two wires through the bottom of one group. Pull wires down, and tape together.

2 Using floral adhesive, glue two overlapping rows of *Gladiolus* florets to a cardboard flange.

3 Slide the small composite flower into the opening in the floret-covered flange to complete the bouquet.

The fantasy form of a composite bouquet—a bouquet assembled from flower petals or florets that, when finished, appears to be one large blossom—can be quite striking. A glamellia, crafted from delicate *Gladiolus* florets, is especially impacting. This one is made even more so with the addition of flowing string smilax rather than cascading ribbons.

Although this bouquet is all white and perfect for the bride, glamellias composed from colorful *Gladioli* varieties are equally impressive.

Since composite bouquets do not benefit from a water source, a spray of antitranspirant will help the delicate blossoms retain moisture for a fresh appearance.

materials:

Gladioli
string smilax
Oasis Floral Adhesive
cardboard flange
thin-gauge wire
floral tape

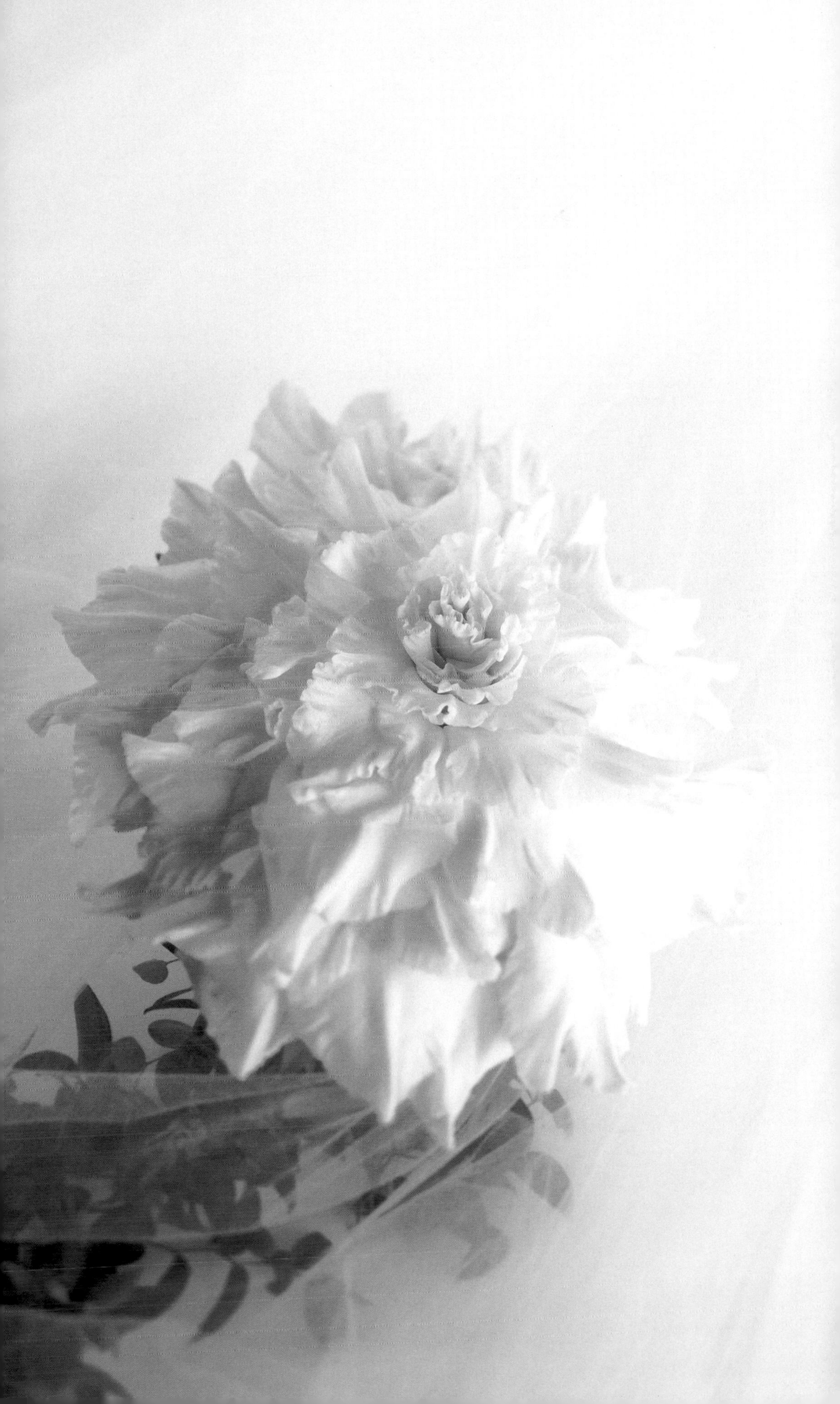

10 ruffled roses

Beautify budding roses with ruffle-edge *Gladiolus* petals.

1 Remove *Gladiolus* florets from their stems. Slice the florets open, and remove pistils and stamens.

2 With floral adhesive, glue several *Gladiolus* petals to the stem of a budding rose, so the petals encircle the bud.

3 Arrange the composite flowers in a bouquet holder, and finish with remaining materials.

Gladiolus florets and budding roses combine to form small ruffle-edge composite flowers. And a collection of several of these pretty *Gladiolus*-enhanced roses forms this elegant bouquet. Swirls of artificial wired vines, artfully wrapped around the bouquet, echo the movement of the lightly scalloped *Gladiolus* petals.

If brighter colors are desired for summer, the many varieties and colors of roses and *Gladioli* available offer numerous design possibilities. And remember that the *Gladioli* will maintain their vibrant appearance longer if treated with antitranspirant.

materials:
roses
Gladiolus florets
star asparagus (*Asparagus deflexis*)
artificial wired vines
Oasis Floral Adhesive
Bouquet Mates bouquet holder

11 duchess rose

Composed of rose petals, this exquisite bouquet is fit for royalty.

Individual petals from 21 roses were used to create this regal bouquet, which is grand enough for brides at the most formal weddings. Seven different varieties—'Avalanche,' 'Mystic,' 'Maureen,' 'Suplesse,' 'Royal Renatta,' 'Danielle,' and 'Peppermint'—were selected for their various colors. Together, the reassembled varieties enable the soft and subtle color transition from light to dark.

A few sprigs of star asparagus (*Asparagus deflexis*) and a sheer, rust-colored ribbon, are all the adornments needed for this spectacular creation.

1 Remove petals from roses. Double-pierce two or three petals at a time with thin hairpin-shaped wires. Twist the wires at the base of the petal cluster.

2 Tape the petal groups in overlapping rows around a single rose blossom until the desired dimension is achieved.

3 Wire sprigs of star asparagus and tape them to the petal cluster. Wrap the wire handle with ribbon, and finish with a bow.

materials:
roses
star asparagus (*Asparagus deflexis*)
ribbon
thin-gauge wire
floral tape

hybrid lily

Oriental lilies are
re-created into one
impressive bloom.

1 Remove the petals from several Oriental lilies. Save the pistils and stamens. Thread a chenille stem through the lower end of each petal, and fold it over.

2 Reassemble the flower in a lily form, frequently taping the chenille stems with floral tape, so they do not slip.

3 Continue adding petals until the desired shape and size are reached. Glue the pistil and stamen into the center of the flower with floral adhesive.

The natural beauty of premium Oriental lilies makes them ideal for wedding use. Capitalizing on their unmatched elegance, this composite arrangement comprises the petals from two exceptional varieties — 'Barbaresco' and 'Lamancha.'

Unlike most composite arrangements, which are assembled with wire and tape, these fragile lily petals are gently pierced with chenille stems and arranged in an oversized lily formation. The lily's characteristic pistil and stamen are glued in after the flower is completed. A hot pink velvet ribbon adds to the wintry feel of this fashionably sophisticated creation.

materials:
Oriental lilies
chenille stems
velvet ribbon
Oasis Floral Adhesive
floral tape

13 rosemary bundle

Fragrant springtime blossoms abound in this floral cone.

1 Remove the leaves from the bottom one-third of the rosemary stems. Gather the partially stripped rosemary into a bunch, and bind with beading wire.

2 Hot-glue a straight-handled bouquet holder into the rosemary bundle. Wrap the bottom portion of the rosemary stems with ribbon to form a handle.

3 Arrange flowers in the bouquet holder. Coil wired vines around the rosemary bundle. String hyacinth blossoms onto beading wire, and wrap the resulting garland around the composition.

Featuring fragrant rosemary and a mix of sweet-smelling blossoms, this pretty cone-shaped bouquet can beautifully grace any springtime wedding, from casual to formal.

To create this luscious selection, the rosemary is formed into a hedge-like bunch and banded together with beading wire. A straight-handled bouquet holder, into which the flowers are arranged, is nestled into the rosemary. Permanent wired vines are coiled around the rosemary hedge, and a garland of hyacinths, strung on beading wire and wrapped around the cluster of florals, echoes the movement of the wired vines.

materials:

roses
hyacinths
rosemary
ribbon
artificial wired vines
beading wire
Wedding Belle Bouquet Holder
hot glue

14 orchid cone

A glorious cluster of *Cymbidium* orchids is showcased in this nature-made cone bouquet. The extraordinary blooms are arranged in an Iglu Holder that rests atop a plastic foam cone. *Galax* leaves, applied in overlapping layers, cover the foam cone. Forming the handle and gracefully coiling around the leaf-covered cone, artificial wired vines rustically enhance the design.

Though typically associated with formal events, the collection of chartreuse-colored, premium *Cymbidium* orchids is perfectly comfortable in this nature-tailored bouquet.

1 Spray the back-sides of *Galax* leaves with adhesive. Place the leaves onto the foam cone in overlapping layers, so that the foam is completely covered.

2 Coil artificial wired vine around the leaf-covered cone. Twist more of the wired vine to form a handle, and secure it into the plastic foam cone with hot glue.

3 Hot-glue a saturated Iglu Holder atop the foam cone. Arrange orchids in the Iglu Holder.

materials:

Cymbidium orchids
Galax leaves
artificial wired vines
plastic foam cone
Oasis Iglu Holder
hot glue
Tack 2000 spray adhesive

15

exotic beauties

A leaf-covered cone showcases some of nature's finest orchids.

1 Apply spray adhesive to the front sides of *Hypericum* foliage. Place the leaves, back-side out, onto the foam cone in overlapping layers, until the cone is completely covered.

2 Attach two plumes of *Eucomis* to wired picks, and, with beading wire, join the plumes together at the top to form an arching handle.

3 Hot-glue a bouquet holder into the center of the plastic foam cone. Place florals into the saturated foam.

Unparalleled in their beauty, wonderfully exotic lady's slipper orchids (*Paphiopedilum*), complemented by the captivating shapes of geranium foliage, are arranged atop a leaf-covered plastic foam cone. Wired together at their peaks, two plumes of *Eucomis* are attached to picks, which are inserted into the foam cone to form the handle.

Hypericum foliage, the back-sides of which are an autumnal russet hue, are applied, with their colorful back-sides out, to the plastic foam cone with spray adhesive, adding an outdoorsy feel to the radiant fall composition.

materials:

lady's slipper orchids
Eucomis
geranium foliage
Hypericum foliage
Wedding Belle Bouquet Holder
plastic foam cone
Tack 2000 spray adhesive
beading wire
wired picks
hot glue

flowering hedge

Myrtle makes a wonderful winter green. Here, it is gathered with Japanese boxwood and trimmed to form a flat-topped hedge-like bundle into which pristine *Stephanotis* blossoms are arranged. The collection, fabulous for a winter wedding, requires little ornamentation—only the silver paddle wire that encircles the bare portion of the foliage bundle.

Stay-Fresh Stephanotis Stems, which keep the star-shaped blossoms looking fresh throughout the event, also make easy work of the stemming process. To ensure that the blooms last as long as possible without wilting, they may be immersed in an antitranspirant solution prior to assembly.

1 Remove the leaves from the bottom one-third of the foliage stems. Gather the partially stripped foliage into a bunch, and bind it with silver paddle wire.

2 Trim the top of the foliage bundle in hedge-like fashion.

3 Attach Stay-Fresh Stephanotis Stems to the *Stephanotis* blossoms. Glue the stemmed blossoms into the foliage hedge with floral adhesive.

materials:

Stephanotis blossoms
myrtle
Japanese boxwood
Stay-Fresh Stephanotis Stems
Oasis Floral Adhesive
silver paddle wire

hanging tulips

With modern updates, this stylish bouquet has classical roots.

Dual focal points are established in this creative arrangement, which showcases a stunning collection of *Phalaenopsis* orchids accented by lovely pendulous tulips. Blades of lily grass, around which copper beading wire has been elegantly wrapped in a crisscross pattern, also drape from within the orchid gathering and join the two focal areas.

Although markedly different from traditional cascades, this modern composition is up to date in its presentation yet classic in its materials and grandeur, so it will suit many brides' tastes and style preferences.

1 Insert tulips into the bouquet holder, so they hang in a downward-facing position.

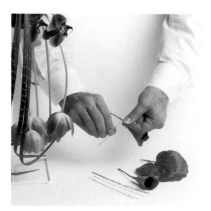

2 Wrap blades of lily grass with copper wire in a crisscross manner. Add the wire-wrapped lily grass into the bouquet.

3 Roll *Galax* leaves into small "funnels." Wrap the rolled leaves with thin-gauge wire. Insert the orchids, and add the leaf rolls to support the blossoms.

materials:

Phalaenopsis orchids
tulips
Galax leaves
lily grass (*Liriope*)
Wedding Belle Bouquet Holder
copper beading wire
thin-gauge wire

florals nouveau

Today's in-demand
florals revamp the
traditional cascade.

1 With floral adhesive, glue hanging *Amaranthus* into the base of a bouquet holder.

Contemporary materials, including hanging *Amaranthus*, ornamental kale, and blooming basil, propel the cascade style into the 21st century in this monochromatic selection. The graceful curves of miniature callas and variegated *Aspidistra* add movement to the design and further elevate its modern-day appeal.

To accomplish the curved appearance, the stems of the miniature callas are rubbed and shaped by hand several times until the stems maintain the arching curves. When sliced into strips, the *Aspidistra* leaves naturally flex into a slight curl.

2 Slice an *Aspidistra* leaf into several strips. Place the strips into the bouquet holder.

3 Rub and gently flex the miniature calla stems until a curving shape is achieved. Add the callas to the design.

materials:

roses
miniature callas
ornamental kale
lily grass (*Liriope*)
hanging *Amaranthus*
blooming basil
variegated *Aspidistra*
Wedding Belle Bouquet Holder
Oasis Floral Adhesive

grain cascade

Vine wreaths and hanging millet accessorize this bouquet.

Millet, suspended upside down from the base of an autumn-inspired gathering of *Liatris*, Matsumoto asters, and *Camellia* foliage, forms a contemporary fall cascade. Some of the long, fluffy *Liatris* spikes, jutting from the base of the design, help to visually connect the central cluster of blossoms with the downward-facing millet.

Within the symmetrically arranged flower cluster are two vine wreaths, which add dimension to the design. Because of their color, the wreaths coordinate with the millet and help to form a visual connection between the blossoms and the pendulous grains.

1 Bind a grouping of millet with waterproof tape. Hook the bundle with heavy-gauge wire, and insert the wire into the bouquet holder. Bend the wire over the top of the bouquet holder.

2 With heavy-gauge, hairpin-shaped wires, attach the two vine wreaths, in overlapping fashion, to the bouquet holder.

3 Arrange the floral materials, placing some of the elements to conceal parts of the vine wreaths.

materials:

Matsumoto asters
Liatris
Camellia leaves
millet (*Setaria*)
vine wreaths
Oasis waterproof tape
heavy-gauge wire
Bouquet Mates bouquet holder

20 flowing lilies

Nontraditional cascading materials form an up-to-date bouquet.

1 String spruce cones onto beading wire to form a garland.

2 Attach the cone garland to almost-leafless ivy vines.

3 Coil organza ribbon around the cone-enhanced vines, securing the ribbon in place with beading wire.

The cascade style can be modernized for contemporary brides with up-to-date florals such as the exquisite Oriental lilies used here. The ragged-edged gold mesh ribbon and trailing strands of cone-adorned ivy also set this bouquet apart.

Arranged in a bouquet holder, some of the lilies are placed in a small cluster while others dangle from the grouping in cascading fashion. Miniature spruce cones, attached to loosely foliated vines and accessorized with strips of metallic organza ribbon, also fall from the bouquet's central area. The entire composition is backed by a ragged-edged piece of mesh ribbon that has been painted gold for the winter season.

materials:
'Nayona' lilies
ivy
miniature spruce cones
metallic organza ribbon
gold-painted mesh ribbon
beading wire
wood picks
Wedding Belle Bouquet Holder

parlor fan

1 Lay *Hydrangea* florets face down, and spray with adhesive.

A charming bridal alternative with Southern flair.

Covered with *Hydrangea* blossoms and ivy leaves, this affordable antique cardboard fan, available in several shapes and sizes from local antique dealers, lends charm to a springtime nuptial celebration.

This two-sided wedding accessory, which is reminiscent of an old-time Sunday social, is ideally suited for a less formal daytime event, but with its Southern styling, this floral fan could easily be carried at evening weddings, especially those showing Southern influence.

Although *Hydrangeas* are available in an assortment of springtime shades, many other types of florets and flower petals could be used to cover the antique fan.

2 Wait a few seconds for the adhesive to become tacky. Then, apply *Hydrangea* florets to the fan in overlapping rows, covering the entire paddle area on both sides.

3 Lay ivy leaves face down, and repeat the gluing process. Apply them in overlapping layers to the handle.

materials:
Hydrangea florets
ivy leaves
cardboard fan
Tack 1000 spray adhesive

22 summer's glory

A formal summer bouquet with a regal handle treatment.

1 Clip tips of *Liatris*, and dip the stem ends into floral adhesive. Glue the *Liatris* into a bouquet holder, filling out the fan shape.

2 Tightly mass orchids in two groups— one on either side of a straight-handled bouquet holder.

3 Cut off the end of the bouquet holder. Using floral adhesive, glue *Liatris* into the handle. Wrap the shortened handle with ribbon.

This stunning two-sided floral fan, arranged in monochromatic color harmony with lavender *Liatris* and *Cymbidium* orchids, is beautifully suited for formal summer weddings. With its ribbon-wrapped, scepter-like handle, which is tipped with a *Liatris* blossom, this elegant fan will make any bride feel like royalty, but it's also perfect for her entire entourage.

Both *Liatris* and *Cymbidium* orchids are available in white. So for brides who desire traditional bouquets composed only of white flowers, these varieties may be substituted.

materials:
Liatris
Cymbidium orchids
satin ribbon
Wedding Belle Bouquet Holder
Oasis Floral Adhesive

23 autumn fanfare

Feathers and flowers are the perfect fall combination.

1 Wrap the handle of a straight-handled bouquet holder with brown floral tape. Add pheasant feathers and bind with gold beading wire.

2 Insert a line of pheasant feathers into the foam in an arching manner. Fill in the fan shape with additional materials.

The textures and colors of fall are captured in this bountiful fan-shaped bouquet, which is designed in a straight-handled bouquet holder. Feathers, bound with gold beading wire, disguise and elongate the holder's handle.

A variety of materials could be used to create such a bouquet, but pheasant feathers are seasonal staples, and the miniature callas add the golden-yellow and orange hues of autumn. Because callas' stems are soft and supple, they are glued into the foam rather than just inserted into it. For the most fresh presentation, the callas should be added on the day of the event.

3 Dip the miniature calla's stems in floral adhesive, and place them in the arrangement.

materials:

miniature callas
Crocosmia
Solidaster
dried *Protea latifolia*
pheasant feathers
Wedding Belle Bouquet Holder
Oasis Floral Adhesive
brown floral tape
gold beading wire

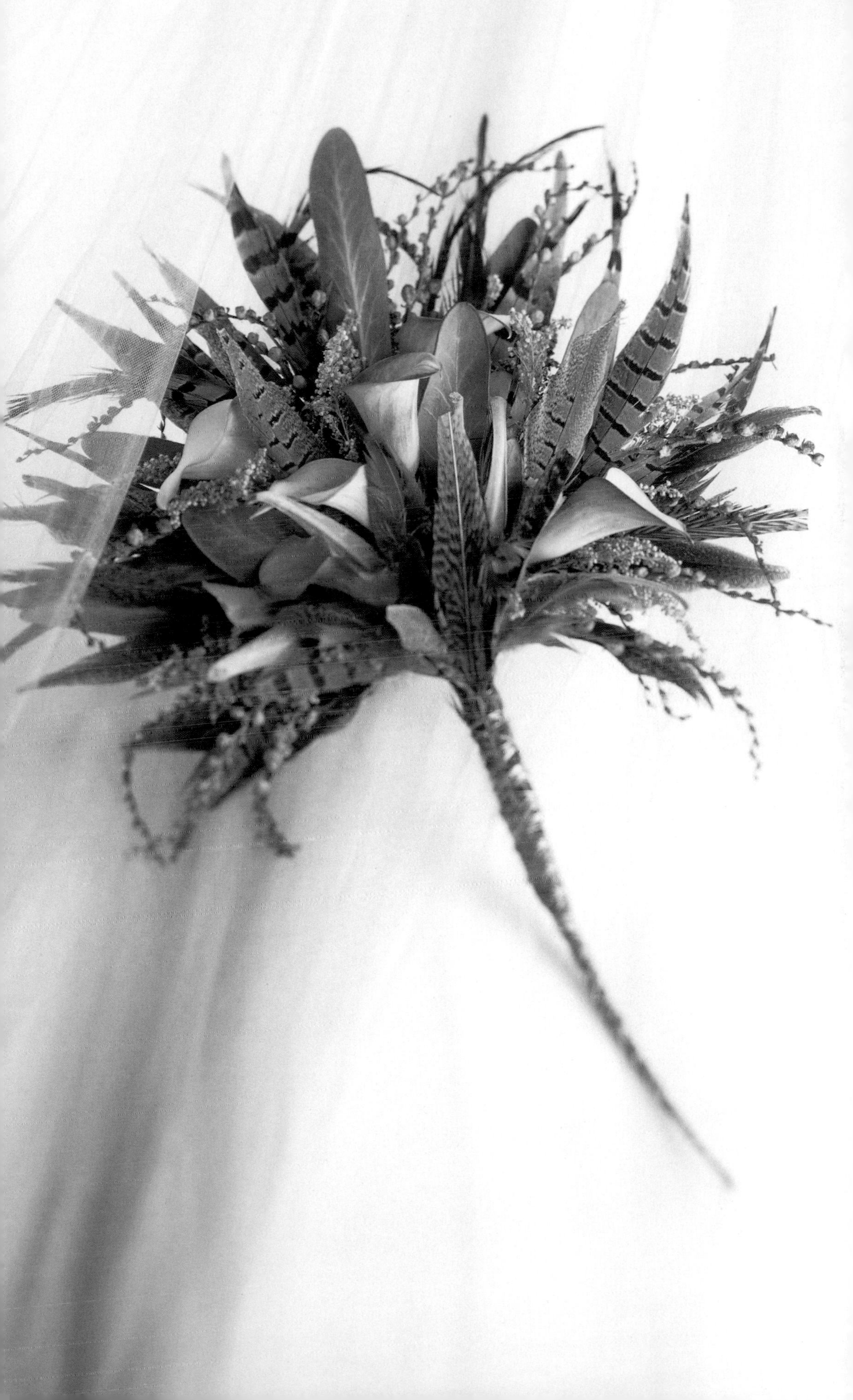

holiday dazzle

A dramatic fan
bouquet decked out
for the holiday season.

Ornate holiday ornaments and a bejeweled golden handle distinguish this lovely bouquet, which is designed for a wedding held during the holiday season. The flat ornaments, glued to each side of the floral fan, coordinate with the golden wrapping of ribbon on the handle. A small plastic jewel is attached to the end of the handle to finish it with style.

This bouquet's sophisticated stylings make it grand enough for the bride as well as her maids and could even be carried by the mother of the bride.

1 Cut 10 lengths of heavy-gauge wire, and cover each with floral tape. Shape one piece of wire into an arch. Twist the ends of the other pieces around the arched piece to begin forming the fan shape.

2 Bring the ends of the nine pieces together, and bind with tape. Insert the fan-shaped brace into the bouquet holder. Arrange the statice in the foam, and bind the statice to the wire brace with raffia.

3 Glue in the remaining materials with floral adhesive. Wrap the handle with ribbon, and glue a plastic jewel to the end. Glue two flat ornaments, one on either side, at the base of the fan.

materials:

'Misty Blue' statice
heather (*Erica persoluta*)
Grevillea
Wedding Belle Bouquet Holder
two flat ornaments
plastic jewel
ribbon
raffia
wire
floral tape
hot glue
Oasis Floral Adhesive

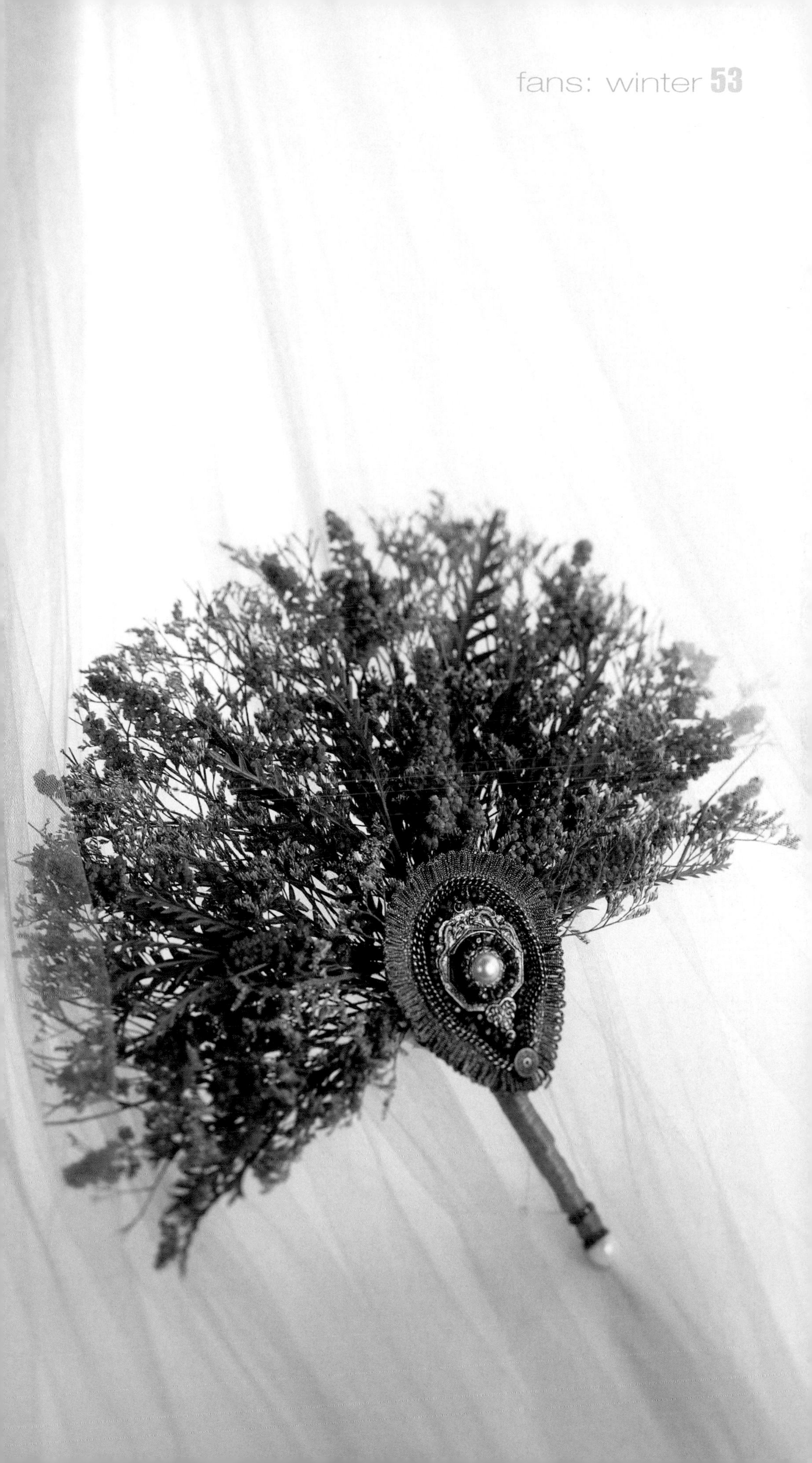

25

Iris basket

A woven mat enwraps an *Iris* bundle in this architectural creation.

1 Assemble the foliage into parallel rows.

In a tall, woven design, this springtime collection of pretty purple *Irises* makes an exceptionally striking bouquet for brides and maids. The natural, handmade bouquet holder, which looks like a tall basket or woven vase, is made from both *Dietes* and *Crocosmia* foliage that has been partially woven into a mat. The mat is simply wrapped around a tall bundle of *Irises*, which are banded at the base, and secured with boutonniere pins.

Serving as foliage accents, the unwoven ends of the mat surround the blooms, which are gathered into a single-level, hedge-like bunch.

2 Weave additional blades of the foliage into the lower two-thirds of the parallel rows to form a partially woven mat. Use floral adhesive to secure the foliage at the edges of the mat.

3 Assemble a bunch of *Irises* so the blossoms are all at the same height. Bind the grouping with waterproof tape. Wrap the *Irises* with the mat, and secure the mat in place with boutonniere pins.

materials:

Irises
Dietes foliage
Crocosmia foliage
Oasis Floral Adhesive
Oasis Waterproof Tape
boutonniere pins

Dense vines are made more airy for light, flowy accents.

1 Arrange florals in a bouquet holder. Gently separate stands of string smilax from the bunch.

2 Clip off some of the leaves, so the vines are loosely foliated.

A gorgeous cluster of Oriental lilies and white roses is transformed into an elegant cascade with the addition of string smilax, variegated ivy, *Chlorophytum*, and variegated buckthorn (*Rhamnus*).

For an airy foliage treatment, which prevents the flowers from being overshadowed by dense vines, some of the leaves have been removed from the smilax string. The less foliated vines are light and diffuse and radiate, in elegant tendrils, from the floral cluster.

Especially useful for wedding arrangements, this technique could be applied to any densely foliated material but is most effective with trailing vines.

3 Add foliages in trailing and spraying formations.

materials:
'Time-Out' lilies
roses
Bupleurum
variegated ivy
string smilax (*Asparagus smilax*)
Chlorophytum
variegated buckthorn (*Rhamnus*)
bouquet holder

Magnolia collar

Magnolia leaves, with their sienna-hued back-sides facing outward, form a fabulous fall collar for this bounteous bouquet of roses, *Hypericum* berries, *Gerberas*, pincushion proteas (*Leucospermum*), and yarrow.

The orange-brown hue of the leaves, which are simply stapled to a premade satin bouquet collar that is designed to slip onto a bouquet holder, is just right for accommodating the floral materials. And with their delightfully exotic formation, as well as their golden hue, the pincushion proteas are excellent additions to this autumnal grouping.

1 Staple *Magnolia* foliage, back-side out, to a satin bouquet collar until the collar is completely covered.

2 Drop a saturated bouquet holder into the center of the leaf-covered collar.

3 Arrange florals in the foam in a mounded formation. Add a few backward-facing *Magnolia* leaves into the floral grouping.

materials:

'Peach Surprise' spray roses
Gerberas
Hypericum berries
pincushion proteas (*Leucospermum*)
cottage yarrow
Magnolia leaves
Syndicate Sales satin collar
Bouquet Mates bouquet holder
stapler and staples

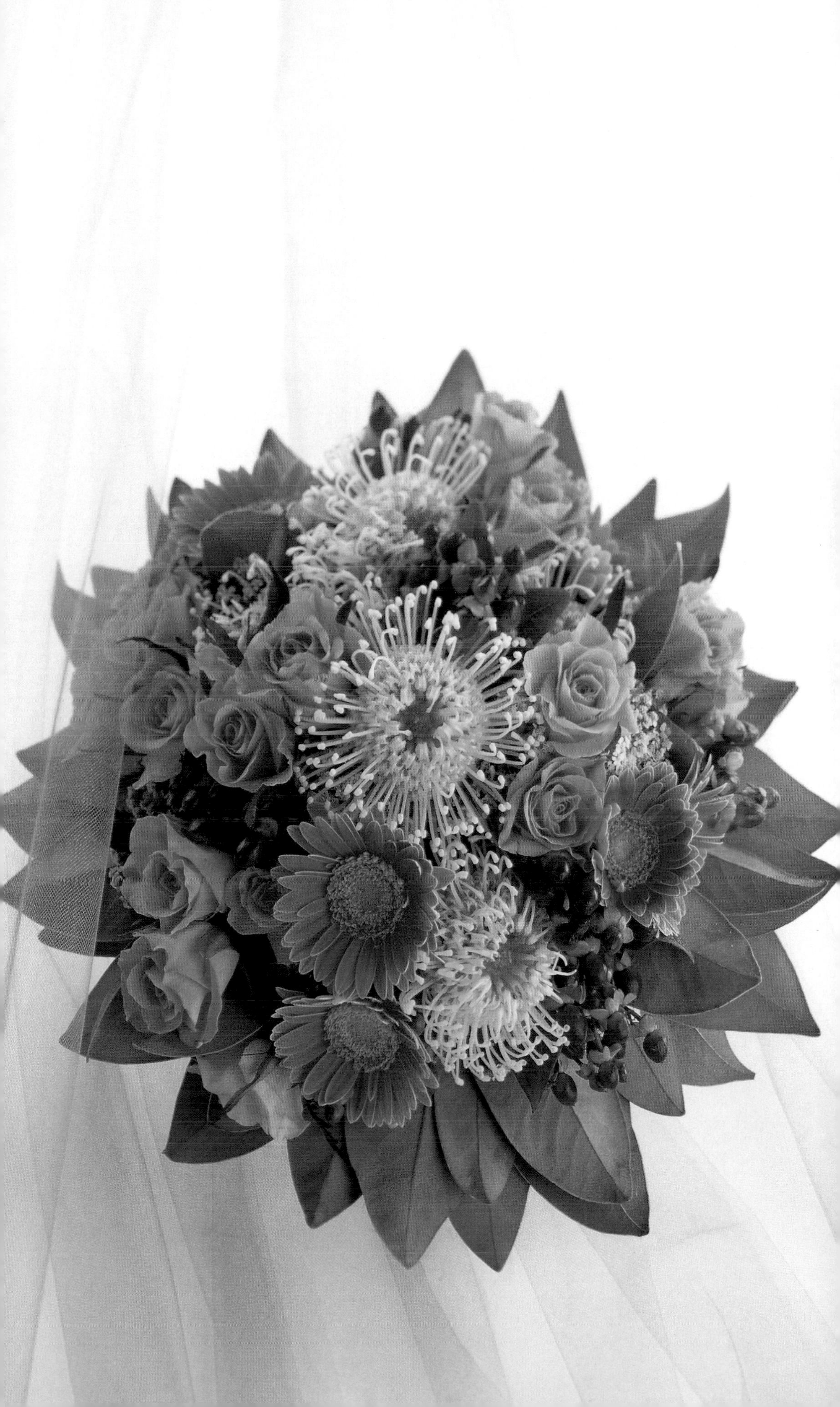

frosted ivy

Table salt achieves an icy effect in this winter wedding selection.

1 Spray ivy leaves with adhesive. Wait a couple of seconds for the glue to become tacky.

2 Sprinkle salt onto the adhesive-covered ivy. Shake off the excess salt. Repeat the process until the leaves are completely covered.

3 Arrange floral materials in a bouquet holder. Accessorize with "frosted" foliage.

'Crystal Lady' lilies are accented by "frosted" foliage and snowberries to create this impressive wintry bouquet, which is absolutely fabulous for December and January nuptials.

The captivating "frosted" foliage is ivy that has been sprayed with adhesive and winterized with a covering of table salt. The easy-to-do frosted effect is the key to this creation's cold-weather application and combines beautifully with the winter-white snowberries and silvery-pink lilies.

Discolor (*Leucadendron discolor*), an unusual spiking foliage, fills out the bouquet's rounded shape and adds an interesting texture to the wintry composition.

materials:
'Crystal Lady' lilies
snowberries
miniature waxflower
ivy
discolor (*Leucadendron discolor*)
bouquet holder
Tack 2000 spray adhesive
table salt

tinted ribbon

Floral paint helps to make a perfect match.

Distinguished by its wide, Dior-style bow, which is tinted green with translucent floral paint to complement the bouquet's pretty pastel hues, this lush and rounded gardeny mix is an excellent choice for the style-conscious bride and her attendants.

Adding movement to the composition, which features roses, *Gerberas*, stock, lisianthuses, waxflower, and more, ivy vines gracefully encircle the florals, which are arranged in a bouquet holder. The wide, green-tinted bow is attached to a wood pick and secured in the foam of the bouquet holder.

1 Tint a wide, cream-colored ribbon by spraying the matte side with hydrangea-green floral paint.

2 Allow the paint to dry, and then tie a two-loop Dior-style bow. Cut a "V" into the end of each streamer.

3 Arrange flowers in a bouquet holder. Add a collar of swirling ivy vines, and insert both ends of the ivy into the foam.

materials:

'Porcelina' roses
Gerberas
lisianthuses
waxflower
stock
Bupleurum
white lace flower (*Didiscus*)
variegated ivy
Just For Flowers hydrangea-green
   floral paint
ribbon
bouquet holder
wood pick

30 untamed sheaf

1. Arrange flowers in a straight-handled bouquet holder. Apply double-stick tape to the handle. Bind a bunch of rose stems with waxed twine, and nestle the bouquet holder into the center of the stem bunch.

2. Tightly wad up a length of satin ribbon. Continue to wad and crumple the ribbon until it maintains a wrinkled appearance.

3. Spread out the crumpled ribbon. With the matte side facing out, so the crumpling is most visible, tie a multiloop bow.

Wild grasses enhance a multidimensional rose composition.

With the look of a hand-tied summer sheaf, this eye-catching bouquet is arranged in a holder that has been nestled into a tightly banded bunch of stripped stems. Arranged amid pretty peach 'Versillia' standard roses and 'Cream Gracia' spray roses, a somewhat unruly assortment of wild grasses lends a slightly untamed, gardeny feel to the structured composition.

The bow, created from satin ribbon, is given a textured look through repeated crumpling. The matte side, or the back-side, is tied to face outward, clearly revealing the faux texture.

materials:

'Versillia' standard roses
'Cream Gracia' spray roses
ti tree foliage
assorted grasses
satin ribbon
Wedding Belle Bouquet Holder
waxed twine
double-stick tape

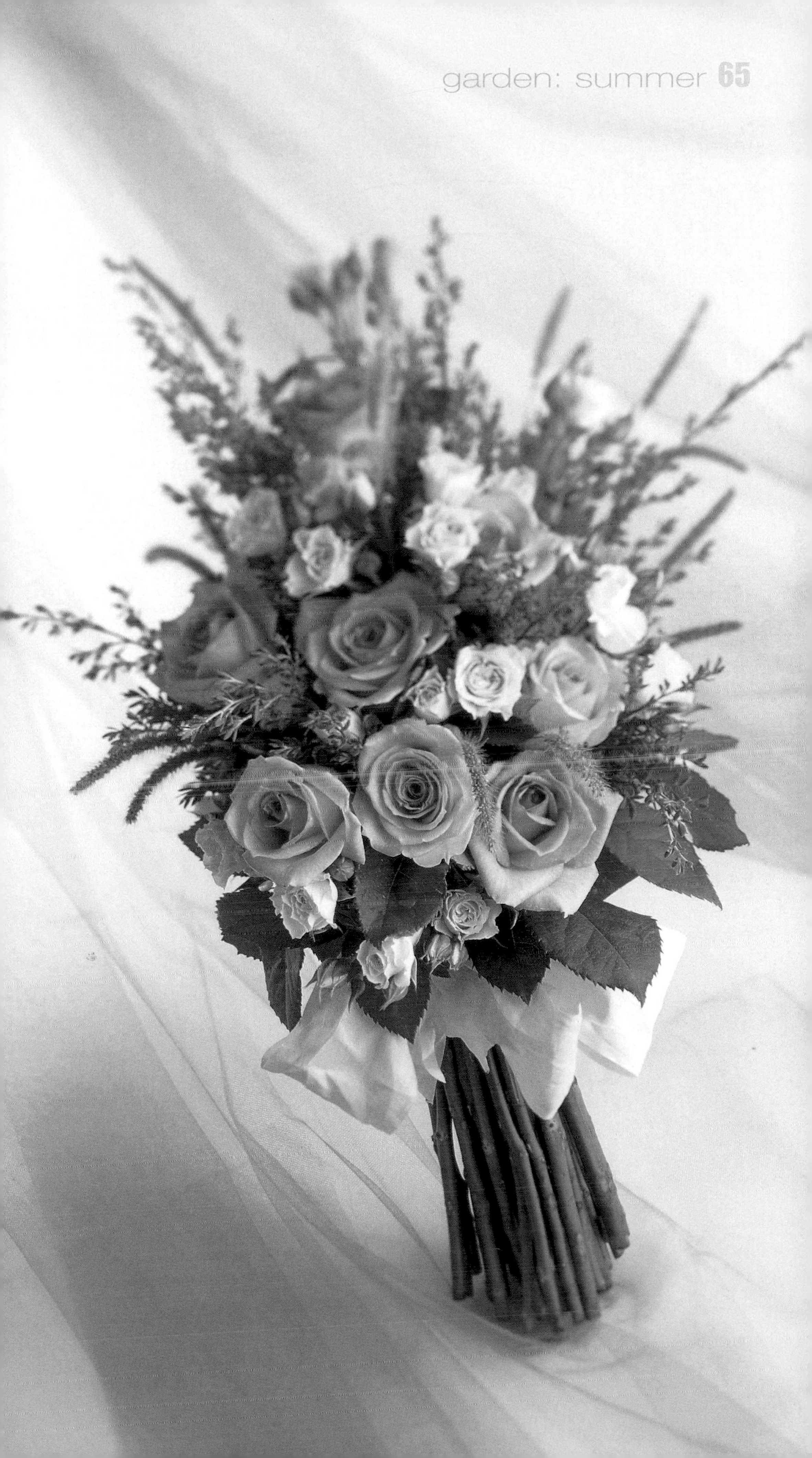

downy nosegay

Feather wreaths and orbs add warmth for autumn weddings.

Decorating these flowers like fabulous boas, two premade feather wreaths, one at the base and one woven among the blossoms, warm this creation for cool-weather weddings. Coordinating with the wreaths, two pinion-covered orbs are arranged amid the florals.

Lending to the bounteous fall presentation, which includes roses and lisianthuses, are two colors of *Hypericum* berries, *Crocosmia*, and *Leucadendron*. *Gerbera* centers—or *Gerbera* blossoms from which the petals have been removed—add an unexpected look.

1 With sturdy-gauge wire wrapped in floral tape, create a "stem" for the feather-covered orbs. Hand-tie the bouquet, and nestle the small feather wreath into the flowers as they're being arranged.

2 Bind the flowers' stems with waterproof tape. Attach taped-wire "stems" to the large feather wreath, and drop the bouquet into the center of the wreath.

3 Bind the flower stems and the taped wires into a single unit with waterproof tape. Coil cording around half the length of the stems, and secure the cording with boutonniere pins.

materials:

roses
Mariachi lisianthuses
Hypericum berries
Crocosmia
'Safari Sunset' *Leucadendron*
Gerberas
feather orbs and wreaths
cording
sturdy-gauge wire
floral tape
Oasis waterproof tape
boutonniere pins

Two bromeliads highlight this all-white gathering.

1 Apply a spot of floral adhesive to one end of a double-pointed pick. Impale each cluster of the short-leafed *Tillandsia* onto the glue-spotted end of the pick. Secure it to the pick with a wrapping of floral tape.

2 Separate the longer *Tillandsia* into individual leaves. Form the ends around a wood pick, and secure the leaves to the pick with floral tape.

3 Place the foliage groupings into the bouquet so that one accents the central cluster and the other serves as flowing foliage streamers.

A winter-white arrangement of tulips, spider *Gerberas*, and silver *Brunia* features nontraditional foliage accents supplied by two types of *Tillandsia*, commonly known as air plant. The flowing foliage, along with a pair of suspended tulips, elongates the nosegay into an elegant cascade and lends a somewhat tropical feel.

Both of these species of *Tillandsia* are categorized as bromeliads and are generally sold as potted plants. To incorporate them into the design, bits of one are impaled onto double-pointed picks and inserted into the central cluster while the other, which features longer, flowing leaves, is separated and taped onto wood picks and added to the bouquet in cascading placements.

materials:
tulips
spider *Gerberas*
silver *Brunia*
Tillandsia
Bouquet Mates bouquet holder
double-pointed wood picks
Oasis Floral Adhesive
floral tape

33 regal groupings

Flowers and foliages flow from a cluster of vivid spring blossoms.

Placed into the bouquet holder in small groupings, the vibrant purple florals, which form an explosion of intense color, are beautifully accented by the soft hues of lavender *Freesia* blossoms. Together, the regal flowers, accented by the flowing materials, compose an enticing bouquet that will coordinate with gowns of nearly any spring hue.

Spraying from within a glorious cluster of purple blossoms, the cascading materials, which include *Delphinium* spikes, ivy, star asparagus (*Asparagus deflexis*), and lily grass (*Liriope*), transform an essentially round bouquet into a fabulous spring cascade.

1 Arrange flowers in a bouquet holder. Apply spray adhesive to the back-sides of ivy leaves, and apply the leaves to the underside of the bouquet holder, so none of the white plastic is visible.

2 Coil thin-gauge wire along the length of the ivy vines, so the vines can be gently curved into pleasing formations.

3 Attach groups of lily grass to wired picks. Insert the lily grass bunches into the bouquet, so the grasses cascade from the base of the design.

materials:

'Purple Sensation' *Irises*
Freesias
Veronica
Delphinium
star asparagus (*Asparagus deflexis*)
lily grass (*Liriope*)
ivy
Wedding Belle Bouquet Holder
Tack 1000 spray adhesive
wired picks
thin-gauge wire

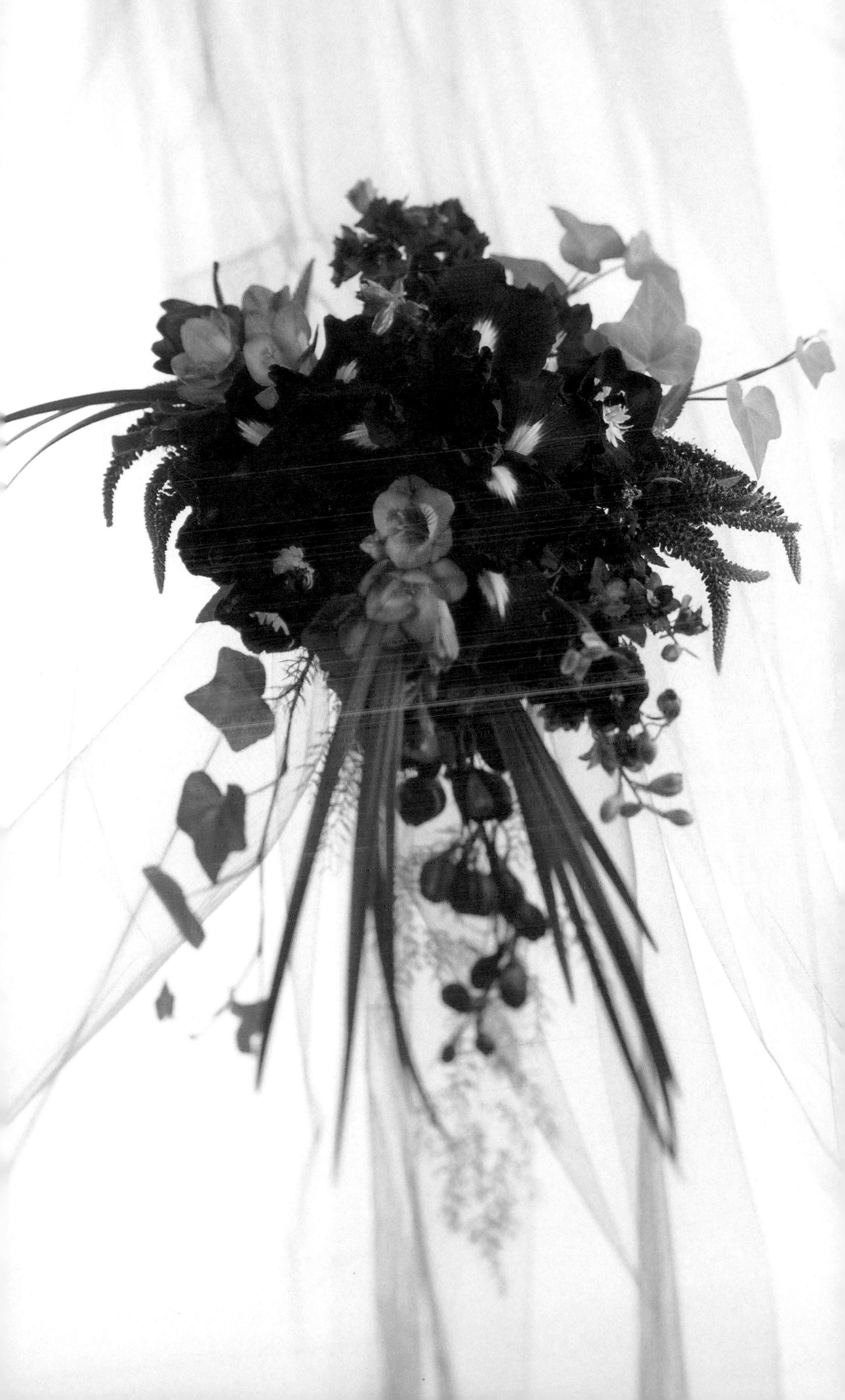

34 trailing vines

Ivy decorates and supports a gardeny mix of materials.

Bands and loops of vining ivy are part of the mechanics in this lush, texture-rich creation. For example, the bouquet holder is wrapped with ivy vines to conceal the plastic. And arranged *en masse*, the gardeny mix of materials, which includes roses, *Gerberas*, *Dahlia*s, *Freesias*, lisianthuses, and more, are inserted into the bouquet holder through a "web" of ivy that is formed by arching ivy vine placements.

Along with flowing ribbon that has been interspersed among the vines, ivy streamers trail from the bouquet to form the glorious summer cascade.

1 Insert strands of ivy around the perimeter of the bouquet holder. Coil these vines around the sides and base of the holder to conceal the plastic.

2 Build an ivy "web" by placing several vines into the bouquet holder in arching placements. Arrange the florals through the ivy "web."

3 Add ribbon and ivy streamers in cascading placements.

materials:

'Surprise' spray roses
waxflower
lisianthuses
miniature *Gerberas*
Bupleurum
Dahlias
Freesias
variegated buckthorn (*Rhamnus*)
ivy
ribbon streamers
Wedding Belle Bouquet Holder

lily cluster

Magnolia foliage complements a *Magnolia*-like formation of lilies.

Such a pristine collection of white lilies needs little ornamentation, but a few well-placed foliage accents can turn a nosegay into a fabulous cascading bouquet. Here, *Magnolia* leaves, some of which are placed so their autumn-hued back-sides are visible, echo the placement of the lilies, which are arranged to resemble a single *Magnoli*a blossom.

Appropriate to the autumnal presentation, a trio of artificial wired vines, braided and coiled into a long swirl, offers a new twist on the traditional ribbon accessory as well as introduces a new and interesting texture to the composition.

Arrange *Magnolia* leaves in a bouquet holder in cascading formation, placing many of them so their brownish back-sides are visible.

Add lilies into the design. Place the blossoms so they appear to form one large *Magnolia*-like bloom.

Braid three strands of artificial wired vine. Coil the braided vines into a swirl, and insert it into the design.

materials:

white 'Stargazer' lilies
Magnolia leaves
artificial wired vines
Bouquet Mates bouquet holder

36 kale rosettes

Reflexed kale centers lend a gardeny feel to this wintry design.

1 Place the ming fern into the bouquet holder in cascading fashion. Remove the rose-like centers from within the ornamental kale blossoms.

2 Reflex some of the outer petals of the kale blossoms, so they resemble open roses. Add the kale centers and other florals to the design.

3 Coil variegated ivy around the central cluster of flowers. Coil additional ivy vines, from which most of the leaves have been removed, around the flowers. Allow some of the tendrils to cascade beneath the blossoms.

The centers of several miniature ornamental kale, the petals of which have been reflexed so that the blossoms resemble small open roses, compose this impressive monochromatic creation.

The florals, which also include roses, snowberries, hyacinths, and miniature *Gerberas*, are arranged amid tufts of ming fern (*Asparagus myriocladus*) and trailing tendrils of variegated ivy, which have been coiled around the central cluster of flowers. Additional ming fern fronds, along with leafless ivy vines also coiled around the all-white blossoms, form the elegant cascade.

materials:

ornamental kale
roses
miniature *Gerberas*
snowberries
hyacinths
variegated ivy
ming fern (*Asparagus myriocladus*)
Wedding Belle Bouquet Holder

1 With floral tape, secure a thin-gauge wire to the stems of several *Camellia* leaves.

2 In your hand, arrange the tulips into a rounded, sphere-shaped formation.

3 Form a collar around the tulips with the wired *Camellia* leaves. Bind the grouping with waterproof tape. Clip the ends of the wires, and cover the tape with ribbon.

Mature tulips naturally form a fabulous rounded bouquet.

An incredible sphere-shaped cluster of lovely peony tulips, hand-tied and accessorized with *Camellia* foliage, makes a fetching bouquet for a variety of springtime events. And since tulips are available in a multitude of types and hues, many different looks can be created with this simple composition.

The round, ball-shaped formation is naturally achieved with mature tulips, the stems of which continue to grow and arch gracefully after they are cut. When the curved stems are hand-gathered *en masse*, the cheery spring blossoms easily form a rounded creation.

materials:
peony tulips
Camellia foliage
ribbon
Oasis waterproof tape
thin-gauge wire
floral tape

38 posy square

1 Spray-paint a chip-wood box and a wooden candlestick with basil-green paint.

2 Once the paint has dried, hot-glue the candlestick to the underside of the chip-wood box.

3 With hot glue, secure a saturated foam cage into the center of the chip-wood box. Place peonies into the foam in a rounded formation.

An unconventional posy holder showcases a peony bouquet.

Contrasting with the square platform upon which it rests, this dazzling mound of fragrant peonies, some of the season's most enchanting blossoms, is beautifully displayed in this unforgettable, romatic creation. The complementary color scheme, achieved with green paint applied to the squared posy holder, further distinguishes the pretty pink mound.

Hot-glued inside the square platform, which is a small chip-wood box, a saturated foam cage holds the exquisite peonies. A wooden candlestick, which serves as the handle, is hot-glued to the chip-wood box to complete the unconventional posy holder.

materials:
peonies
Aquafoam cage
chip-wood box
wooden candlestick
Basil paint
hot glue

total ellipse

A bounty of autumnal materials forms this disk-shaped bouquet.

This contemporary bridal selection, a strikingly elegant floral disk, is laden with a wealth of fall materials and textures. A profusion of tightly massed 'Million Stars' baby's breath supports the florals while a multilayer covering of vines, beading wire, and rawhide strips secures everything in place. Fresh, wire-wrapped wheat adds color and unexpected texture to the covering.

The shapely bouquet offers an unusual yet attractive composition, and its theme can be carried through to the rest of the wedding décor for a complete presentation.

1 Tightly mass a large bunch of 'Million Stars' baby's breath. Band the grouping with waterproof tape. Trim the blossoms into a disk shape.

2 Place the florals into the baby's breath form. Wrap water-soaked vines from a small vine wreath around the perimeter of the disk. Wrap wheat with beading wire, and add it to the perimeter wrappings.

3 Finish the composition with a layer of gold beading wire to secure the materials in place. Add strips of yellow rawhide around the disk's perimeter.

materials:
'Million Stars' baby's breath
Hypericum berries
Echinacea
Crocosmia
annual *Scabiosa*
seeded *Eucalyptus*
kangaroo paws
wheat
small vine wreath
beading wire
rawhide
Oasis waterproof tape

pavé cylinder

A papier-mâché box is transformed into a captivating floral form.

1 Lay spikes of heather atop a papier-mâché cylinder, and bind the blossoms to the cylinder with silver paddle wire. Trim the heather close to the cylinder so that it resembles a low-pile carpet-like covering.

Covered with tiny pink heather blossoms and bound with paddle wire, a basic papier-mâché cylinder holds an impressive collection of bicolor carnations arranged in pavé fashion. Coiled atop the heather-covered cylinder are *Casuarina* whips, made by binding the Australian pine-like foliage with paddle wire. Inside, a saturated foam cage keeps the blossoms well hydrated, so this bouquet can be made in advance if necessary.

A wooden candlestick, embellished with a wooden egg and painted silver, is inverted and glued to the bottom of the cylinder to form the design's unusually attractive handle.

2 Hot-glue the egg into the open end of the candlestick. Paint the egg-topped candlestick with silver spray paint. Once the paint has dried, apply hot glue to the bottom of the candlestick, and adhere it to the papier-mâché cylinder.

3 Line the cylinder with plastic, and insert a saturated foam cage. Arrange the carnations in the cylinder in pavé style. Bind *Casuarina* with silver paddle wire, and coil the wired whips atop the cylinder.

materials:

standard carnations
heather
Casuarina
papier-mâché cylinder
Aquafoam cage
wooden candlestick
wooden egg
Super Silver spray paint
silver paddle wire
hot glue
plastic liner

41

saved stems

Brides get a hand-tied look with a built-in water source.

A bounty of spring blooms appears hand-tied in this pretty bridal design. However, the florals are arranged in a bouquet holder, so a water source keeps them looking fresh for the duration of the ceremony and reception. A stem handle covering, slipped over the bouquet holder's straight handle, results in the hand-tied appearance.

Tied in French twists, a pastel-hued, sheer ribbon adorns the stems and provides additional binding to hold them in place.

1 Arrange flowers in a bouquet holder. Wrap handle with double-stick tape. Clean saved flower stems, and bind them with waterproof tape. Slide bouquet holder into stem bundle.

2 Tie ribbon in a French twist around the stems by wrapping the stems, crossing the free ends of the the ribbon, and twisting them against themselves.

3 Attach a chenille stem to a bow made of sheer ribbon. Push the chenille stem into the foam of the bouquet holder.

materials:

L.A. hybrid lilies

French tulips

spray roses

waxflower

Freesias

blue lace flower (*Didiscus*)

lavender

variegated ivy

star asparagus (*Asparagus deflexis*)

Wedding Belle Bouquet Holder

ribbon and chenille stems

Oasis waterproof tape

double-stick tape

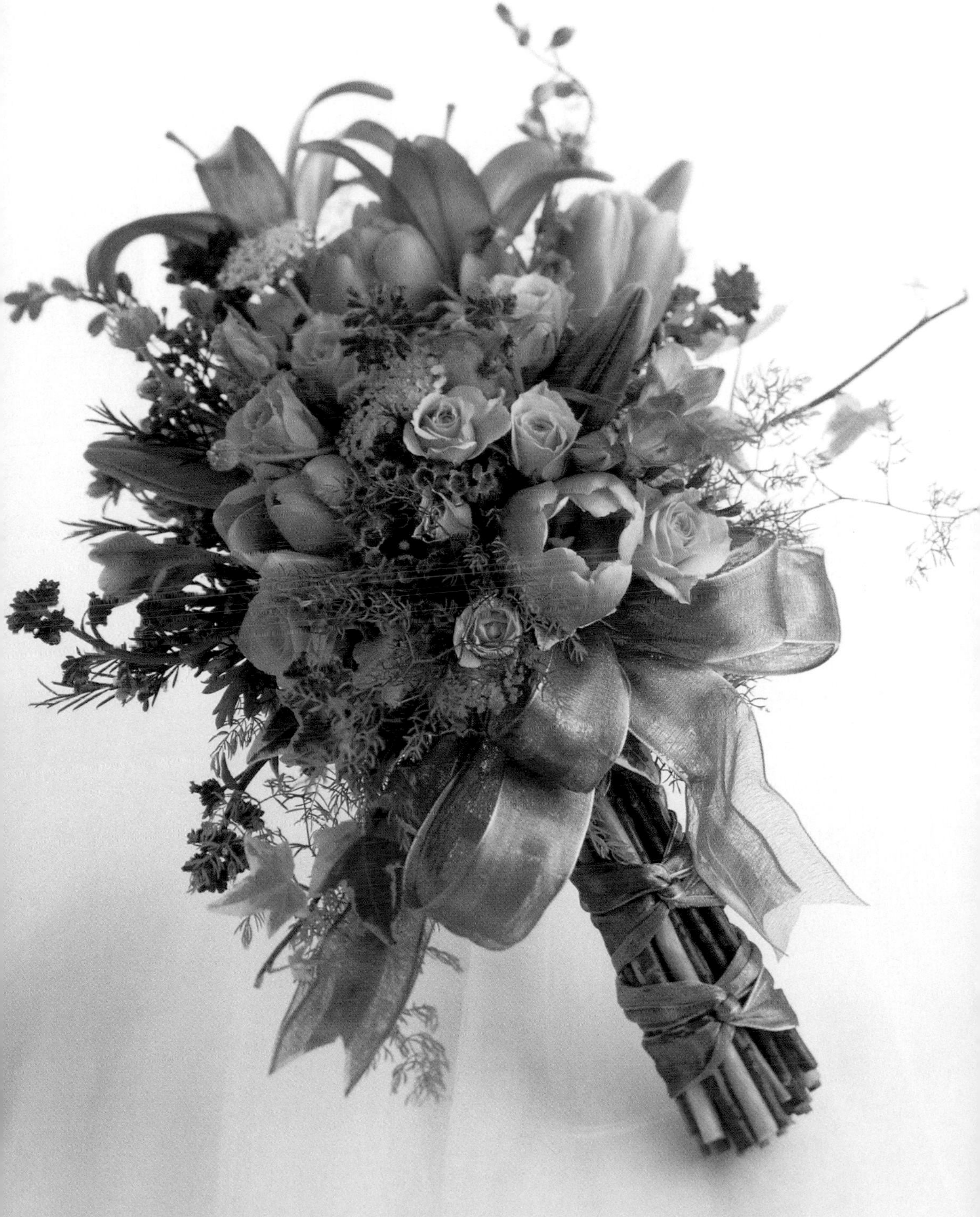

42 "fern-tastic" handle

1 Insert foxtail fern into each of the openings in the Designette's base.

2 Wrap the fern with gold beading wire, creating a handle that looks like a single thick fern frond.

3 Arrange garden roses in the Designette. Use rose leaves as the accent foliage.

Beautiful garden roses are complemented by a foxtail fern handle.

Summer's radiance and glory are captured in these exquisite crimson and pink garden roses—'Ld Braithwaite' and 'Gertrude Jekyll.' Their unmatched beauty and gentle fragrance is showcased in this bouquet, to which a gardeny complement is added with the foxtail, or meyeri, fern (*Asparagus meyeri*) handle covering.

A decorative wrapping of beading wire shapes the foliage into a dense foxtail fern handle and highlights the foliage's interesting texture. The Designette—a foam cage with a short, straight handle—is the perfect mechanic for this natural, fern-handled bouquet.

materials:

'Ld Braithwaite' garden roses
'Gertrude Jekyll' garden roses
foxtail fern (*Asparagus meyeri*)
Designette Floral Design Tool
beading wire

43 wire wrap

From traditional bouquet holder to nature-inspired nosegay.

Barked wire, a permanent vine-like material with a flexible wire center, is the handle treatment of choice for this gorgeous arrangement. Coiled around the bouquet holder's straight handle, the wire's woody appearance transforms the white plastic holder into a nature-inspired nosegay, making it the perfect receptacle for an autumnal bridal accessory.

The floral materials—*Epidendrum* orchids, *Sandersonia*, and foxtail fern (*Asparagus meyeri*)—are beautifully complemented by the rustic wrap. Together, they form a dynamic color story that is ideal for fall wedding fashions.

1 Wrap the handle of a straight-handled bouquet holder with brown stem wrap. Then wrap the handle with double-stick tape. Tightly coil barked wire around the taped handle.

2 Form a small wreath-like structure and several small decorative coils from the barked wire. Place the wire "wreath" onto the bouquet holder, so it tops the barked wire handle treatment. Insert the coils through the "wreath" and into the foam.

3 Clip the foxtail fern into sections, and cover the base of the foam with the cuttings. Then arrange the florals.

materials:

Epidendrum orchids
Sandersonia
foxtail fern (*Asparagus meyeri*)
Wedding Belle Bouquet Holder
barked wire
double-stick tape
brown stem wrap

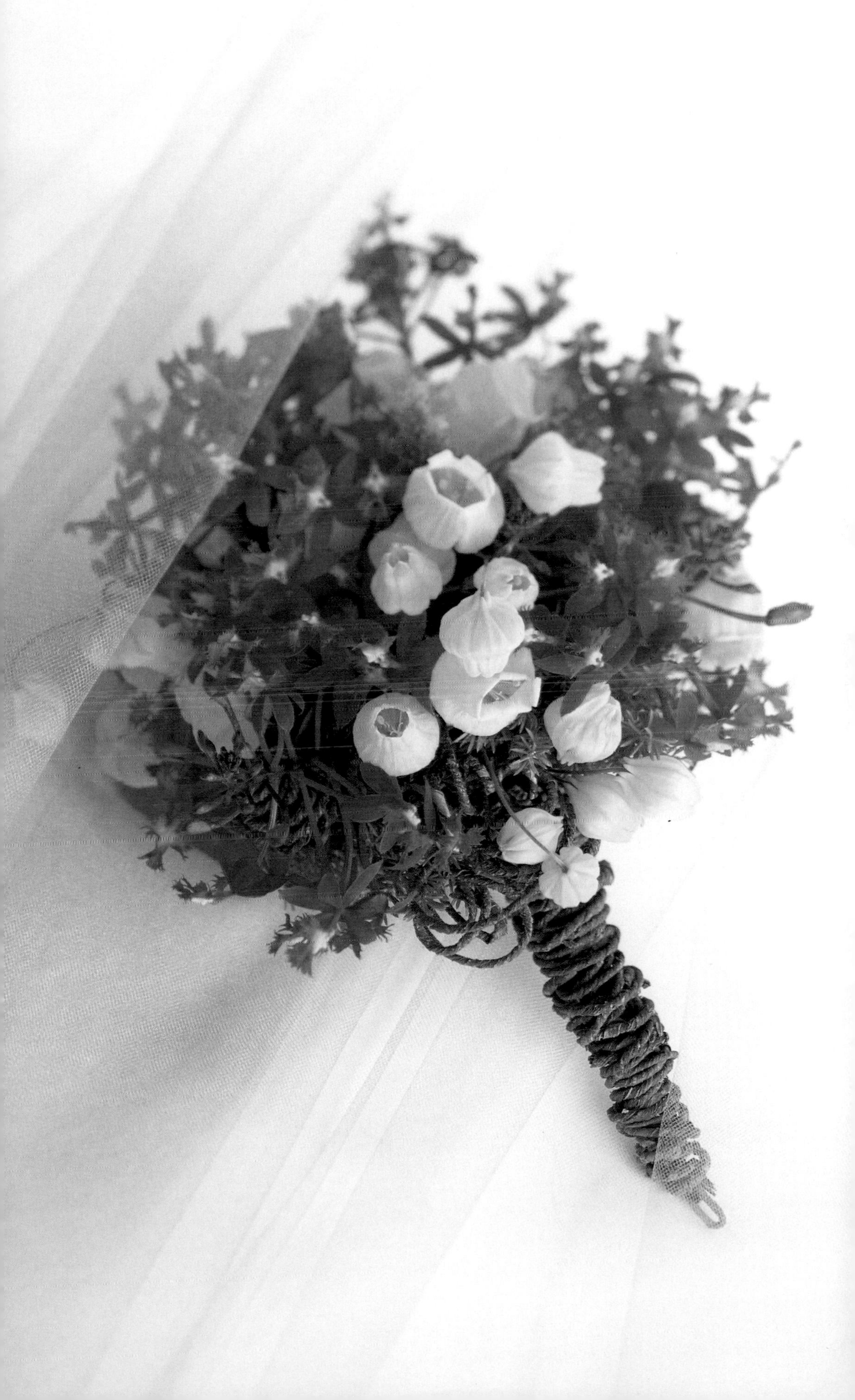

candle holder

A candlestick handle is both decorative and functional.

Highlighted by sumptuous burgundy and yellow 'Hocus Pocus' roses, which are distinguished by their unusual color formations, this enchanting winter wedding creation features a wooden candlestick as its handle. The base of the candlestick is removed, and the plastic handle of the bouquet holder is secured into the open end of the candlestick, providing an attractive and firm grip for brides and maids.

Seeded *Eucalyptus* and miniature spruce cones, along with rose foliage, accent the stunning multicolor roses and add to the bouquet's wintry ambience.

1 Cut off the base of a wooden candlestick. Smooth the cut end with a file.

2 Shorten the handle of a straight-handled bouquet holder. Wrap the short end with enough waterproof tape to hold it firmly inside the candlestick. Wedge the bouquet holder into the candlestick.

3 Coil a chenille stem around the bottoms of the miniature spruce cones to create a spruce cone "pick." Tuck the spruce cones into the arrangement with the florals.

materials:

'Hocus Pocus' standard roses
seeded *Eucalyptus*
miniature spruce cones
wooden candlestick
Wedding Belle Bouquet Holder
chenille stems
Oasis waterproof tape

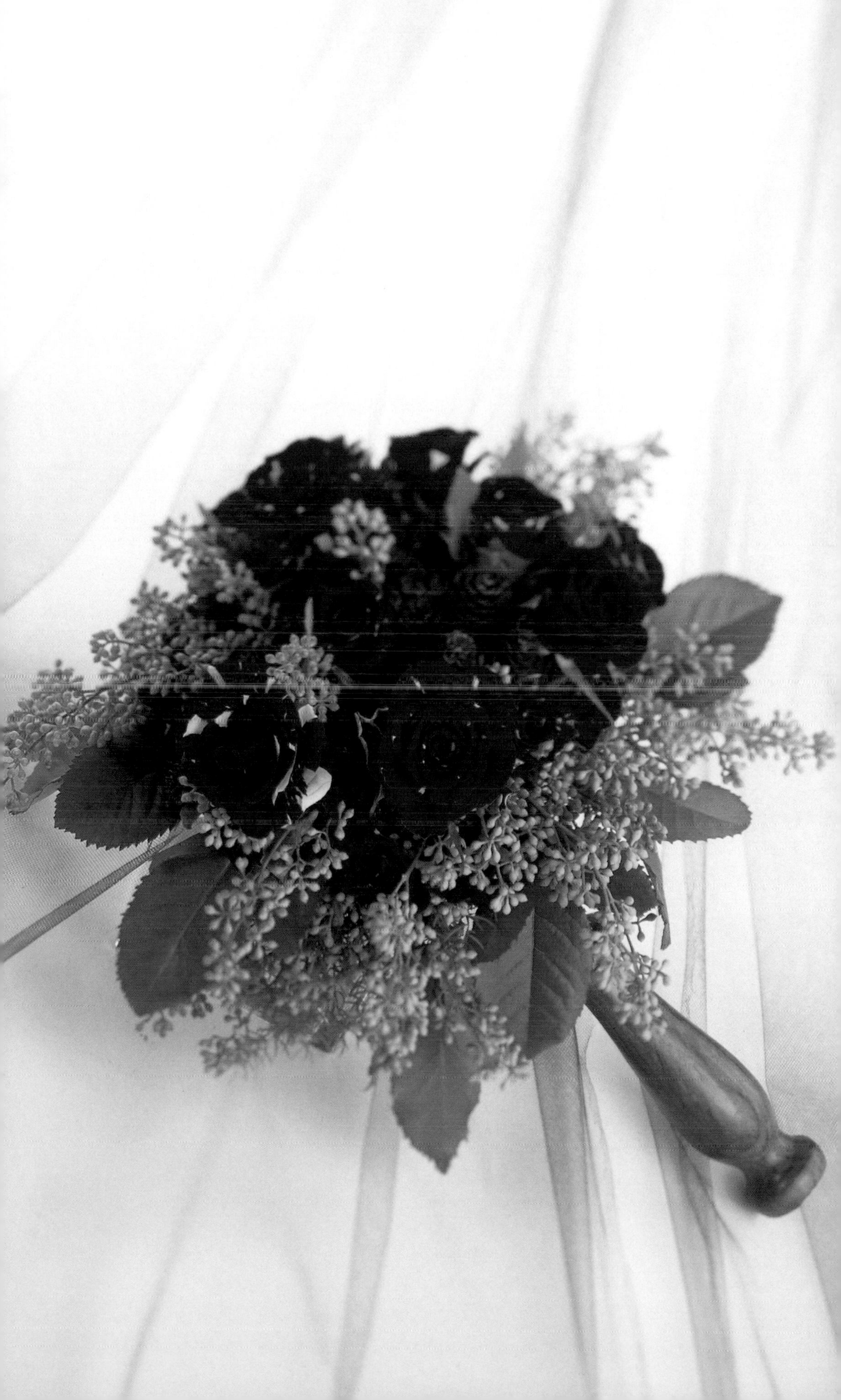

45

casual clusters

Small blossoms are more impacting when arranged in clusters.

1 Remove foliage from the lower ends of the stems. Group the smaller materials into bunches, and add the bunches into the design.

This charming lavender mix, excellent for almost any style of springtime event, comprises roses, *Saponaria*, *Nigella*, waxflower, and more. The hand-gathered design, given a slightly untamed appearance by the *Nigella*, has a casual, carefree feel, but the pretty Dior-style bow embellishes the bouquet for evening or formal affairs.

Greatest impact is achieved by clustering the small-blossomed materials, such as the waxflower and *Saponaria*, into bunches and adding them to the design, which is bound with waterproof tape. Ribbon, held in place by corsage pins, conceals the tape. The wide Dior-style bow finishes the creation with flair.

2 Bind the hand-tied gathering with waterproof tape. Conceal the tape with a band of ribbon. Secure the ribbon with corsage pins.

3 Tie a flat, Dior-style bow. Bind the bow with a chenille stem, and add the center knot. Attach the bow to a wood pick, and insert the bow.

materials:

roses
Nigella
Eucalyptus gunnii
Saponaria
miniature waxflower
ribbon
Oasis waterproof tape
corsage pins
chenille stems and wood picks

46

natural support

Baby's breath serves as the mechanic for this summery mix.

Arranged within a cloud of baby's breath, this colorful, gardeny cluster will coordinate with practically any of summer's most in-demand color schemes. The materials, including garden roses, two colors of *Anemones*, tulips, *Veronica*, blue lace flower, *Campanula*, and more, are tucked into the large tuft of baby's breath, which holds the florals in place. Short-stemmed and thirsty flowers are placed in water tubes and are glued into the baby's breath cluster.

Finishing the design in summery fashion, a hot pink tulle bow is tied to the delightful creation.

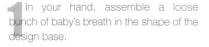

1 In your hand, assemble a loose bunch of baby's breath in the shape of the design base.

2 Insert flowers into the baby's breath framework, allowing them to rest just above the cluster.

3 Place short-stemmed and thirsty flowers in Aquapics, and glue the flower-filled water tubes into the design with floral adhesive.

materials:

garden roses
Anemones
tulips
Veronica
Campanula
blue lace flower (*Didiscus*)
dusty miller
baby's breath
Aquapics
Oasis Floral Adhesive

ribbon collar

Ivy and ribbon embellishments highlight this striking nosegay.

1 Remove foliage from the lower ends of the stems. Place florals into groups, and assemble. Bind the materials with waterproof tape, and conceal the tape with ribbon.

2 Expand the opening in the flange by making one-inch cuts from the center toward the edge of the flange.

3 With floral adhesive, glue two rows of ivy leaves to the flange, Then, staple on the ribbon loops. Drop the bouquet into the expanded flange opening.

Rich in textures and autumnal hues, this fabulous fall mound is distinguished by the many loops of ribbon that grace its perimeter. The loops, made of woven, gold-edged ribbon, are stapled onto a cardboard flange for quick and easy embellishment. Another collar is formed around the bouquet with ivy leaves, two rows of which are glued to the same flange as the ribbon.

The elegant, mixed composition, with its warm earthy tones, is a wonderful autumn option suitable for both brides and maids.

materials:

'Sahara' roses
Scabiosa
Ageratum
Bupleurum
chocolate cosmos
ivy leaves
ribbon
cardboard flange
Oasis Floral Adhesive
stapler and staples

rosemary ring

Seasonal icons transform spring blooms into wintry wonders.

1 Remove the foliage from the lower ends of the stems, and arrange the florals in your hand. Wrap the stems of the hand-tied materials with waterproof tape.

2 Form a wreath-shaped collar from whips of rosemary. Place four long taped wires onto the rosemary ring, and drop the hand-tied arrangement through the ring, incorporating the taped-wire stems into the fresh stem bundle.

3 Just beneath the rosemary ring, coil tasseled cording around the stems, so that the tassel is positioned in the front of the bouquet. Secure the cording with corsage pins.

Many of the materials in this all-white gathering, such as the lilies, *Freesias*, and lisianthuses, would ordinarily be considered among spring's first fruits. But with the addition of wintry materials such as snowberry and rosemary, an aromatic herb, these traditional spring blossoms become ideal winter wedding selections.

The rosemary is used to create a holiday appropriate wreath-like ring that encircles the stems. Tasseled drapery cording, which also encircles the flowers' stems, adds a dressmaker's touch to the late-season collection.

materials:

Asiatic lilies
roses
carnations
lisianthuses
Freesias
Gerberas
snowberries
rosemary
tasseled cording
corsage pins
thin-gauge wire
Oasis waterproof tape
floral tape

Spring-loving daisies are accessorized with pearl-headed pins.

Pearl-headed corsage pins bejewel this happy collection of Marguerite daisies. Dressed in a sunny gingham-checked ribbon, the pearl-centered blossoms, arranged in a framework of baby's breath, can attend any of spring's daytime ceremonies.

Imperfect daisies, with lost or damaged petals, may still be used, *sans* petals. Simply pull off all the petals, and insert a corsage pin into the yellow button-like center. The pearl-enhanced centers add another dimension to the bouquet without the introduction of another type of flower.

A simple coiling of wire-edged organza ribbon, accomplished by curling the ends around a pencil and sliding the pencil out, solves the potential problem of fraying and adds a detailed finish to the bow.

1 Insert corsage pins into the centers of Marguerite daisies.

2 Remove petals from imperfect Marguerite daisies, and insert corsage pins to accessorize the button-like centers.

3 Place the pearl-enhanced blossoms into a tuft of baby's breath. Finish with a tie of gingham ribbon.

materials:

Marguerite daisies
baby's breath
corsage pins
gingham ribbon

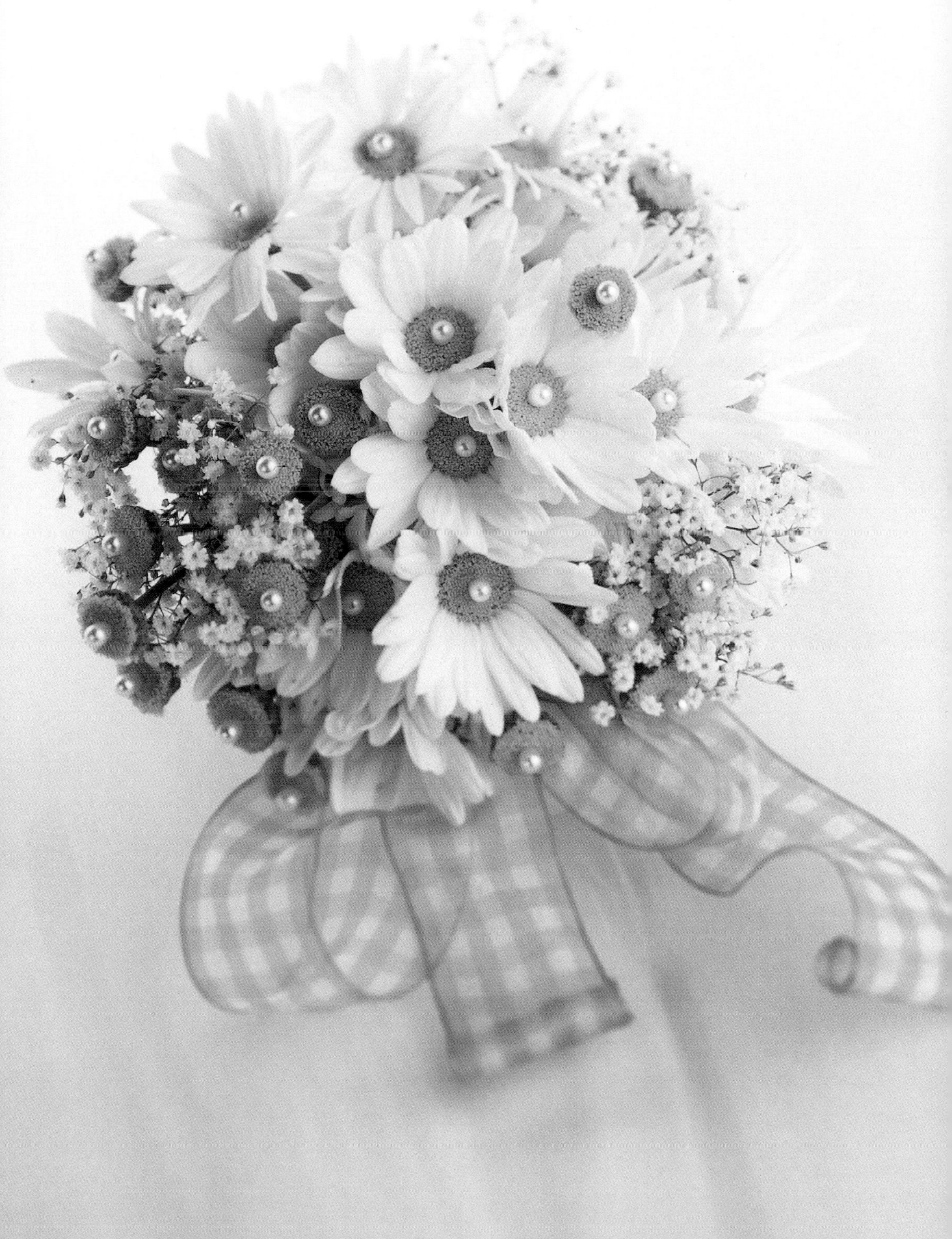

50 jewels of the sea

1 Clip orchid sprays into small sections so that each section contains two blooms. Arrange the short stems and foliage in a saturated bouquet holder.

2 Hot-glue seashells to wood picks. Place the shell-topped wood picks among the orchid blossoms.

3 Cut a length of medium-gauge wire, and form it into a hairpin shape. Slide the hairpin onto the necklace. Insert the wire into the bouquet holder.

Seashells and orchids combine for a fabulous tropical nosegay.

Individual seashells attached to wood picks, as well as a strand of small shells from a seashell necklace, grace this breathtaking summer bouquet, which also features a luxurious collection of *Dendrobium* and *Phalaenopsis* orchids, both of which are exquisite jewels themselves.

Combined with the tropical blossoms, which are accented by orchid foliage placed to elongate the bouquet in cascading fashion, the shells form the heart of this bouquet, which is perfect for a seaside or tropical getaway wedding. The shell necklace replaces the traditional bow and ribbon streamers to complete the presentation.

materials:

Dendrobium orchids
Phalaenopsis orchids
seashells
shell necklace
wood picks
medium-gauge wire
hot glue
Bouquet Mates bouquet holder

51 fine wines

Frayed ribbons tied with jewels showcase fall's delicious hues.

1 Arrange the flowers in a bouquet holder. Remove foliage from ivy, and assemble the vines into a looped grouping. Attach the leafless vine group to wired picks.

2 Insert the long-stemmed chocolate cosmos into the design so they appear to be floating.

3 Tie plastic beads onto the tattered ribbon streamers to complete the jeweled effect.

From blush to burgundy, this intriguing fall bouquet embodies a range of wine-colored hues as well as an assortment of interesting, texture-rich materials. These florals, including roses, callas, chocolate cosmos, *Leucadendron*, and seeded *Eucalyptus*, are arranged in groups for greatest impact.

Jewel-like, plastic beads, tied into tattered-edge ribbons, cascade from the fall collection. A vine treatment, achieved with ivy from which the leaves have been removed, as well as chocolate cosmos placed on the bouquet's edge, add movement to the retro-inspired creation.

materials:

'Blue Curiosa' roses
Sedum
heather (*Erica persoluta*)
miniature callas
chocolate cosmos
seeded *Eucalyptus*
'Safari Sunset' *Leucadendron*
ivy vines
ribbon
jewel-like, plastic beads
Wedding Belle Bouquet Holder
wired picks

gold and pearls

Gardenias are accented with pearls and gold for winter affairs.

A massive *Fatsia* leaf, dusted with antique gold, serves as an easy-to-add edging in this fabulous and fragrant winter wedding design. Composed of exquisite *Gardenias*, this striking bouquet is beautifully accessorized with gold-trimmed clusters of pearls and coordinating pearl-and-gold-enhanced tassels.

Taped to chenille stems, the gold-adorned pearl clusters are easily placed within the bouquet. Chenille stems also make including the *Gardenias* easier. But since these flowers are sensitive and prone to wilting, the stem ends should remain exposed, so they can be inserted into the saturated foam as well.

1 Dust the *Fatsia* leaf with antique gold paint. With floral adhesive, glue the leaf to the back-side of a straight-handled bouquet holder.

2 Tape *Gardenias* to chenille stems, but leave the stem ends exposed, so they may contact water in the bouquet holder and remain hydrated.

3 Disassemble the grape-like clusters of pearls. Create smaller clusters, and bind them together with gold bullion. Insert the clusters, and finish with the tassels.

materials:

Gardenias
Fatsia japonica
Japanese boxwood
Oasis Floral Adhesive
Wedding Belle Bouquet Holder
pearl clusters
pearled tassels
gold bullion
chenille stems
Antique Gold spray paint
floral tape

53 dapper daisies

Casual and carefree for spring.

1 Arrange *Gerberas* in a straight-handled bouquet holder. Save the stems, and coil a length of picot ribbon around each one.

2 Cluster the ribbon-wrapped stems, and bind them with waterproof tape.

3 Cover the tape with ribbon. Slide the bouquet holder into the bound stems. Finish with a bow.

Pretty-in-pink *Gerbera* daisies form a carefree nosegay for spring. Growing in popularity in recent years, *Gerberas*, with their multitude of colors and forms available, can meet many brides' needs.

Gerberas will perform best, and will offer the longest-lasting presentation, if they are arranged with a water source. But for brides who desire a hand-tied arrangement, place the blossoms in a bouquet holder, and use the stems as a handle covering.

A loose wrapping of pink picot ribbon around each of the stems completes the design with an intriguing beribboned effect. Once the stems are gathered together, the individual wrapping ensures that the ribbons are placed evenly among the stems, rather than just around the perimeter.

materials:

Gerberas

ivy

Wedding Belle Bouquet Holder

picot ribbon

Oasis waterproof tape

Delicate pink-flowering
herbs arranged
en masse.

1 Clip the stems short, and arrange the flowers, in a rounded nosegay shape, in a bouquet holder.

Tendrils of *Saponaria* (soapwort) blossoms—a perennial herb whose roots have been used for soap—compose this loosely arranged summer bouquet. Although they appear hand-gathered, the massing of delicate pink flowers is designed in a bouquet holder since *Saponaria* are quick to wilt without a water source. Reserved stems, bundled with floral tape, conceal the bouquet holder's handle and yield the hand-tied appearance.

Complementing the bouquet is a wide bow of sheer, wire-edged ribbon. The loops of the bow have been flattened and the tails curled for a tailored appearance.

2 Wrap the handle of the bouquet holder with double-stick tape. Bind the reserved stems with waterproof tape, and insert the bouquet holder into the bunched stems.

3 Create a large bow with wide, wire-edge ribbon. Flatten the loops, and roll the tails around a pencil. Slide the pencil out to achieve the curled appearance.

materials:

Saponaria
Wedding Belle Bouquet Holder
wire-edged ribbon
double-stick tape
Oasis waterproof tape

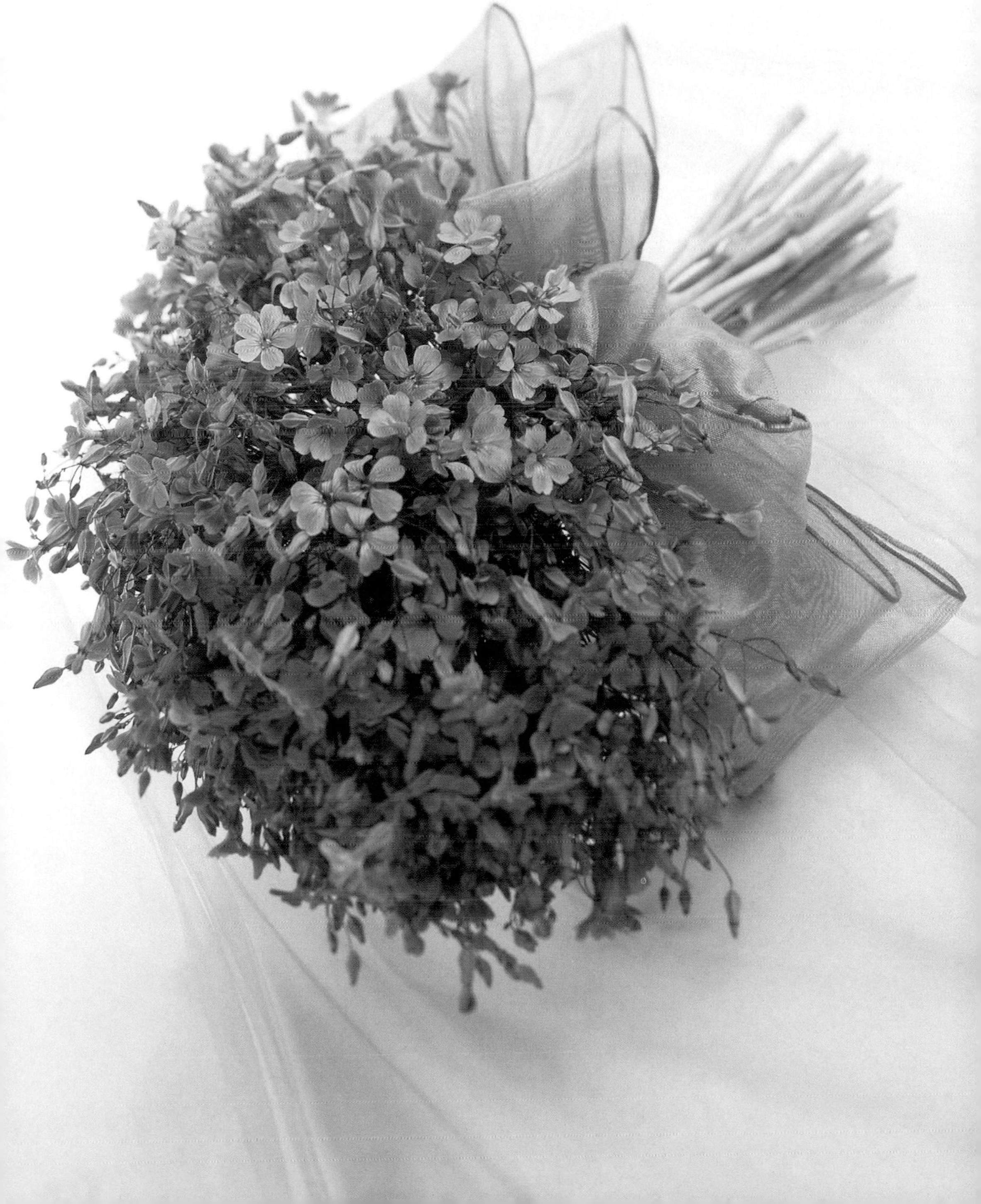

Fall-colored flowers dress up for evening weddings.

A glorious collection of fall-hued *Dahlias*, along with *Dahlia* foliage and buds, is arranged in a bouquet holder that has been adorned with a drapery tassel. Inserted after the blossoms are arranged, the buds offer an interesting textural contrast to the full-petaled *Dahlias*.

A collar of *Galax* leaves, glued to the underside of a straight-handled bouquet holder, results in a completely finished design with no visible plastic. And lending a formal, decorator element, the wood-topped tassel dresses up the design for evening affairs.

1 Wrap the handle of a straight-handled bouquet holder with brown floral tape. Spray *Galax* leaves with adhesive. Apply leaves to the underside of the holder.

2 Slide the bouquet holder into a wood-topped drapery tassel. Secure the bouquet holder to the tassel with hot glue.

3 Finish the design with insertions of *Dahlia* buds among the open blossoms.

materials:

cactus *Dahlias*
Galax leaves
drapery tassel
Wedding Belle Bouquet Holder
brown floral tape
Tack 2000 spray adhesive
hot glue

sweet Freesias

A formal bouquet for the discriminating bride.

1 Staple wedding (asparagus) fern to a flange to form a collar. Insert the bouquet holder into the flange, and glue the flange to the bottom of the holder.

2 Remove open *Freesias* from their bracts, and arrange them in a bouquet holder. Tape *Freesia* buds to chenille stems. Insert the chenille stems into the bouquet holder.

3 Finish with insertions of cascading wedding (asparagus) fern, forming a teardrop shape by adding a tail to the rounded form.

Elegant white *Freesia* blossoms, recognized for their exceptional fragrance, are superior selections for a winter wedding. The mounded creation, arranged in a bouquet holder and accented by a cascade of wedding fern, also called asparagus fern (*Asparagus plumosus*), befits the discriminating bride planning a formal ceremony.

Freesias are available in an array of colors, all of which exude the trademark fragrance. And for attendants, *Freesias* are likely to be available in colors to coordinate with the attire. Whatever the hues, wedding fern will beautifully accent the bouquet.

materials:

Freesias
wedding fern (*Asparagus plumosus*)
bouquet holder
cardboard ribbon flange
chenille stems
hot glue
floral tape
stapler and staples

ringed posy

An all-white Biedermeier nosegay that is just right for the bride.

A vision in white, this structured, Biedermeier-style nosegay, featuring roses, tulips, *Freesias*, and yarrow, is an elegant spring bridal selection. Arranged in a straight-handled bouquet holder, the concentric rings are formed from the inside out, starting at the crown of the holder's foam cage.

Cascading ribbon streamers, tied at the top with bows and wired onto wood picks, adorn the bouquet's edge and disguise the holder's handle. While the streamers add a casual, carefree touch, the ringed, Biedermeier nosegay has a stylized, formal feel.

1 Starting with the innermost group, arrange flowers in rings from the center outward. Tape chenille stems to ivy leaves, and insert the hooks into the foam around the bouquet's edge.

2 Tie multiloop bows, leaving long streamers. Fasten the bows to wired picks, and insert these around the bouquet's edge as well.

3 With waterproof tape, bind the streamers at the base of the bouquet holder. Cover the tape with a band of ribbon, and allow the streamers to hide the handle.

materials:

'Eskimo' roses
tulips
Freesias
cottage yarrow
ivy
Wedding Belle Bouquet Holder
picot ribbon
wired picks
chenille stems
Oasis waterproof tape

Leaf-wrapped roses
are clustered to form
an impacting bouquet.

For a new twist on the standard rose nosegay, these fragrant, sunshine-yellow beauties are individually wrapped with two *Galax* leaves and wired and taped. Each of the leaf-wrapped roses is then assembled into an imaginative, delightfully different summer bouquet for brides and attendants.

To add a little shimmer, this nosegay is enhanced with sprays of 28-gauge silver beading wire that have been attached to wood picks. The wire sprays, added around the edge of the bouquet, form a web-like collar and add movement to the summery composition.

1 Remove the foliage from the roses. Wrap two *Galax* leaves around each rose blossom to form a cone covering. At the base, wrap the *Galax* leaf cone with thin wire to hold the leaves in place.

2 Gather the leaf-wrapped roses into a nosegay. Add a collar of *Galax* leaves around the grouping of leaf-covered blossoms.

3 Attach sprays of silver beading wire to wood picks. Insert the wood picks into the arrangement, so the wire sprays form a web-like collar around the bouquet.

materials:
roses
Galax leaves
28-gauge silver beading wire
thin-gauge wire
wood picks
Oasis waterproof tape

candlelit flowers

1 Hot-glue a glass hurricane or other tall, clear-glass candle holder to the top of an unsaturated bouquet holder.

2 Affix a piece of Cling to the bottom of the pillar, and secure the candle inside the hurricane.

3 Cut off the tip of the bouquet holder's handle. Wrap the handle with ribbon, and bind the ribbon with beading wire. Hot-glue a plastic jewel into the cut end of the handle.

Fruits and florals combine in a citrusy candlelit creation.

A sumptuous collection of 'Queen's Day' roses and miniature oranges, accented by the intriguing forms of *Crocosmia* and millet, are lit for an evening ceremony by a pillar candle placed inside a glass hurricane. The hurricane is affixed to the bouquet holder with hot glue, and Cling holds the candle in place for as long as required.

To finish the design in a manner appropriate to the elegant candlelit presentation, peach ribbon, followed by beading wire, enwrap the bouquet holder's straight handle, and an amber jewel adorns the base.

materials:

'Queen's Day' roses
millet (*Setaria*)
Crocosmia
miniature oranges
candle and hurricane
ribbon
plastic jewel
Wedding Belle Bouquet Holder
hot glue
Cling
beading wire

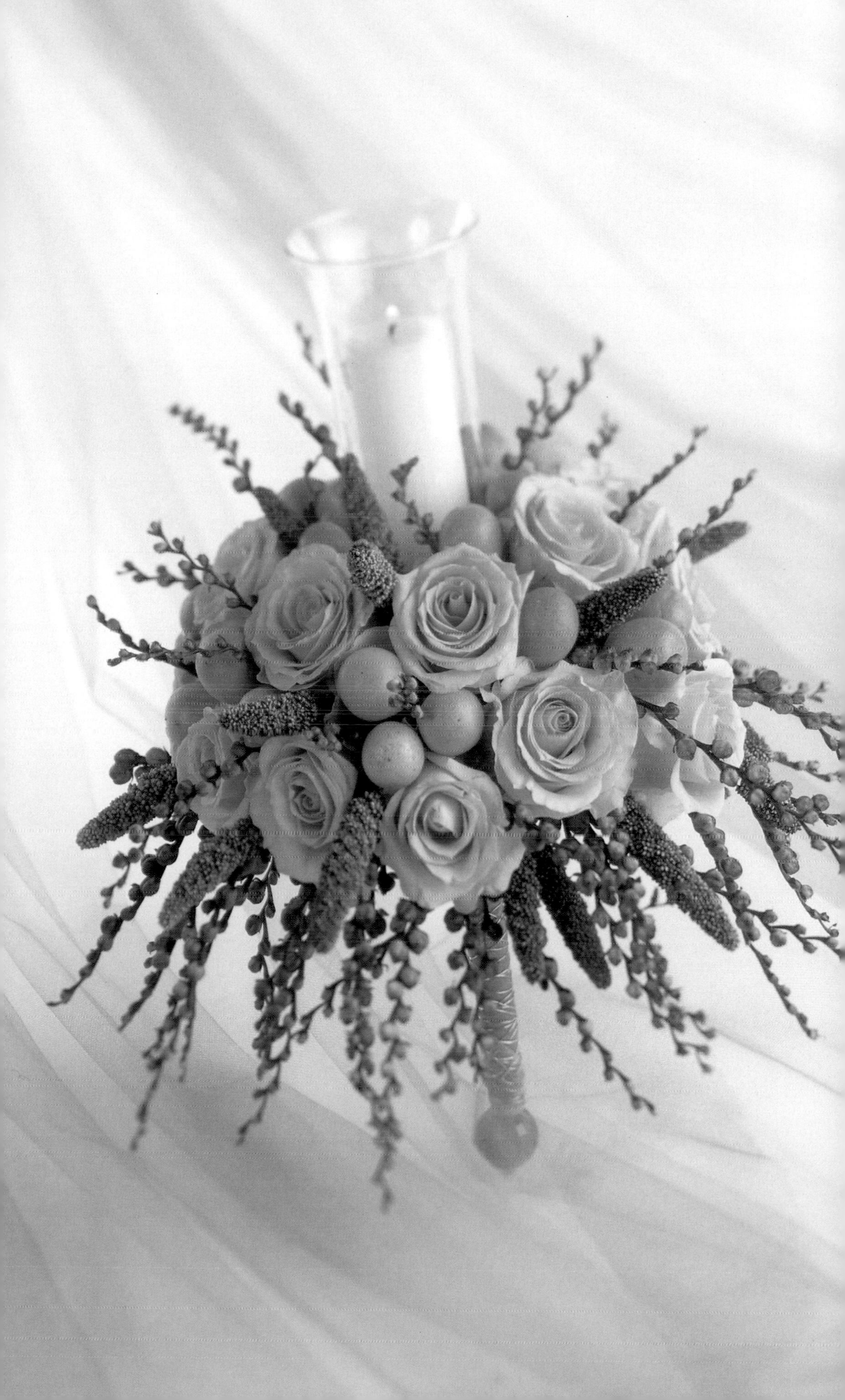

60 rosy starburst

Wrap the handle of a bouquet holder with double-stick tape. Insert the holder into a cluster of *Casuarina*. Bind the cluster with waterproof tape covered with ribbon.

2 Arrange the flowers in the bouquet holder, incorporating the extended *Casuarina* that is attached to the handle.

3 Wire *Casuarina* into small bundles, and insert the bundles into the bouquet holder.

Holiday inspired, this bouquet is ideal for Christmas weddings.

Composed of roses, *Gerberas*, miniature spruce cones, and *Casuarina*, this holiday-inspired nosegay, in traditional reds and greens, makes a striking bouquet for December weddings, especially those scheduled near Christmas.

Long blades of *Casuarina* are adhered to the bouquet holder's straight handle, providing a grassy grip. The starburst effect is achieved with *Casuarina* wired in bunches and placed into the central nosegay of red roses and *Gerberas*. The spraying foliage actually begins at the handle and visually intercepts the design for a dynamic presentation.

materials:

'Ruby Red' roses
'Red Springs' spider *Gerberas*
Casuarina
miniature spruce cones
Wedding Belle Bouquet Holder
double-stick tape
thin-gauge wire
Oasis waterproof tape

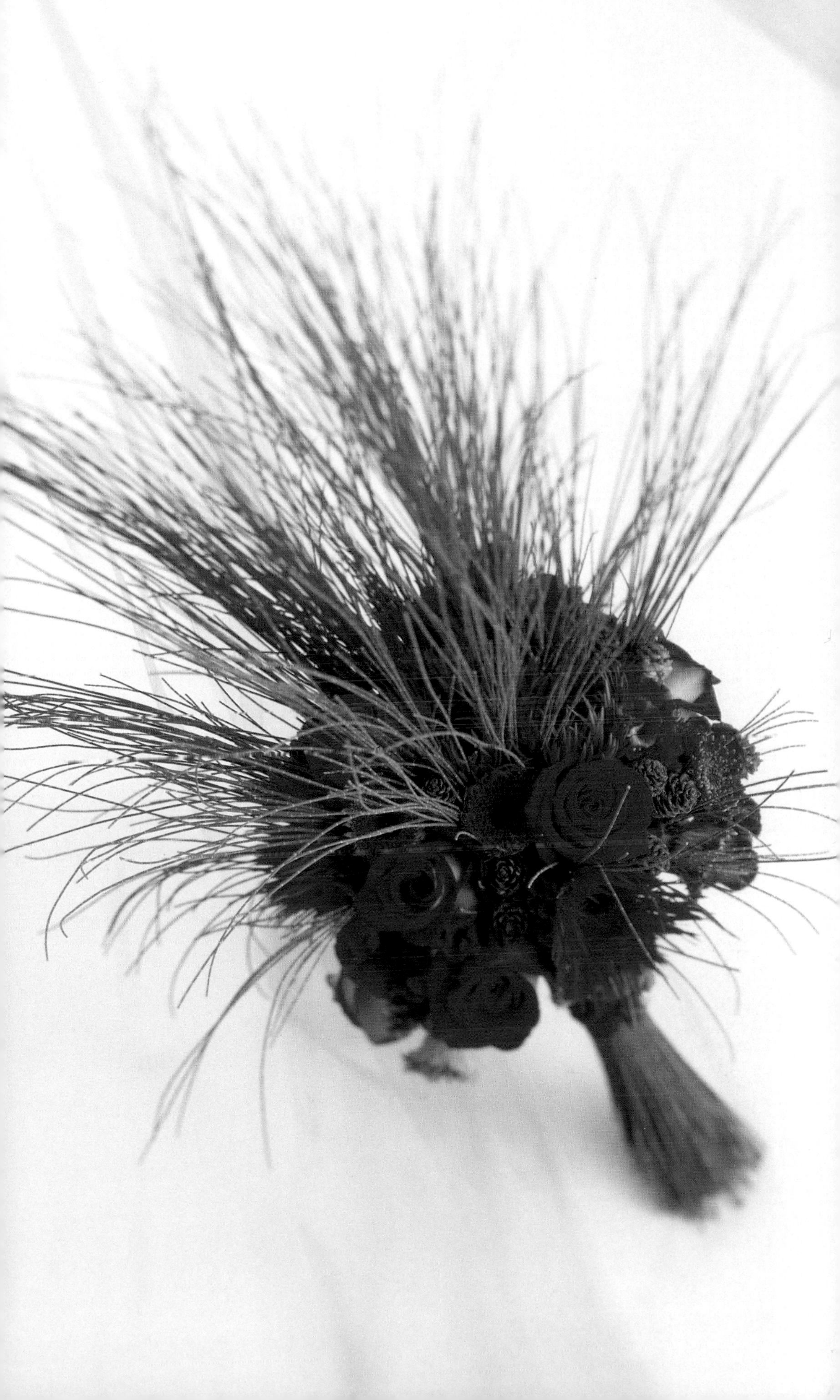

61

spring sphere

A pomander to meet the needs of both bride and flower girl.

This gorgeous collection of spring florals, including *Hydrangea* florets, *Ranunculuses*, waxflower, heather, hyacinths, and *Spiraea*, is wonderful for all the women of the wedding party.

Artfully arranged in two Iglu Holders that have been glued back-to-back, the florals should remain hydrated and intact for a fabulous spring wedding presentation. A webbing of gold beading wire further stabilizes the materials for a long day in the hands of busy flower girls. The beautiful cording handle is created from a length of color-coordinated ribbon that has been wrapped with multiple layers of beading wire.

1 Apply hot glue to the bottoms of two Iglu Holders. Line up the tabs, and press the holders together.

2 Loop a chenille stem through the tabs of the Iglu Holders. Use a dab of hot glue to complete the chenille stem loop.

3 Wrap a wide piece of ribbon with beading wire to create ribbon cording. Loop the cording through chenille loop.

materials:

Hydrangeas
Ranunculuses
Spiraea
waxflower
heather (*Erica melanthera*)
hyacinths
ribbon
beading wire
two Oasis Iglu Holders
chenille stem
hot glue

bell of the ball

1 Clip bells-of-Ireland florets from their stems in groups, leaving the longest stems possible. Place the groups into a saturated foam ball; if necessary, secure the placements with boutonniere pins.

A beautiful summer design for casual or formal events.

Bells-of-Ireland blossoms, removed from their stems in groups, are arranged in a floral foam sphere to create this captivating pomander bouquet. The flowers' unusual chartreuse color will accent gowns, whether brides', bridesmaids', or flower girls', in many summer hues.

A decorative corded tassel, which has been separated into two elements, now serves as the looped handle and the accenting tassel. Both items, the ends of which must be taped to avoid unraveling and water wicking, add a little glamour to this pomander bouquet, making it equally suitable for both casual and formal occasions.

2 Attach the cording loop to a wired pick. Dip the pick's unwired end into floral adhesive, and press the pick into the floral foam ball.

3 Attach the tassel to a wired pick. Dip the pick's unwired end into floral adhesive, and press the pick into the base of the floral foam ball.

materials:
bells-of-Ireland
Oasis floral foam ball
corded tassel
wired picks
Oasis Floral Adhesive
floral tape
boutonniere pins

63 beribboned orb

It's lightweight, sturdy, and stunning for fall.

1 Using several fall-colored ribbons, begin creating a bow. Continue adding loops until a ribbon sphere is formed.

2 Make the final loop extra long to form the pomander "handle." Secure the ribbon ball with a tight central knot.

3 Using floral adhesive, glue the floral materials into the loops of the ball of ribbons.

Rather than being arranged in foam, these lovely fall materials are actually placed within the loops of an oversized bow made from fall-colored ribbons. The flowers' stems are simply dipped into glue and added to the ribbon ball, with the heads of the flowers resting on the tips of the loops.

The various colors and textures incorporated into this bouquet make it easy to coordinate with the bride's color palette. And since the materials are glued in, they should hold fast throughout the celebration. The quick-to-make technique allows the bouquet to be assembled at the last minute while the ribbon base can be made weeks in advance of the event.

materials:
spray roses
Hydrangea blossoms
Sedum
Celosia (cockscomb)
miniature persimmons
bittersweet
Hawthorne berries
Gerberas
ribbon
Oasis Floral Adhesive

asian influence

A rectangular pomander bouquet for Asian-themed events.

1 Cut plastic or dry foam into a rectangular shape. Bore a hole through the length of the foam with a pencil.

2 Thread a length of wire through the hole in the foam and attach it to the corded tassels. Pull the cording through the hole. Form the handle and secure the cording with boutonniere pins.

3 Pin stock florets to the foam brick until the entire surface is covered.

Wonderful for an Asian-themed wedding, this tasseled rectangular pomander is as fragrant as it is beautiful. Its shape, as well as the pretty cording handle and elegant tassels, make it suitable for formal wintertime nuptials.

To create the pomander, the cording is threaded through a brick of plastic foam, and then a wealth of stock florets is pinned to the foam's surface.

Many other types of florals, such as *Delphinium* florets, *Hydrangea* florets, and miniature roses, could be used to cover the surface of the foam brick. Whatever materials are used, a mist of antitranspirant will keep them looking fresh.

materials:
stock florets
corded tassels
plastic or dry foam
boutonniere pins
wire

65

covered purse

Its simple, uncontrived beauty allows the flowers to shine.

1 Cut *Equisetum* in pieces long enough to cover the papier-mâché box. Wrap backward-facing duct tape around the box, so the adhesive side faces out. Affix *Equisetum* to duct tape.

2 Wrap wired vines around the box for extra binding. With dabs of hot glue, affix a permanent vine handle to the inside of the papier-mâché box. Glue a piece of plastic foam into the bottom of the box.

3 Insert *Cymbidium* orchids into Aquapics that have been filled with water. Apply floral adhesive to the end of each Aquapic, and press the Aquapics into the plastic foam.

An *Equisetum* (horsetail) covering transforms a papier-mâché box into a nature-made wedding satchel ideal for bridesmaids and flower girls. If carried by the bride, a blooming vine or a dressing of sheer ribbon could enhance the permanent vine handle to befit the guest of honor.

Whether holding hand-gathered wildflowers or elegant orchid blossoms, such as the *Cymbidiums* shown here, the simple, uncontrived beauty of this purse allows the flowers to truly shine.

Floral purses make the sometimes awkward hand-held accessory a comfortable, everyday item. For flower girls, flower-adorned teddy bears function similarly in that they are comfortable and natural to hold.

materials:

Equisetum
Cymbidium orchids
artificial wired vines
papier-mâché box
duct tape
hot glue
plastic foam
Aquapics

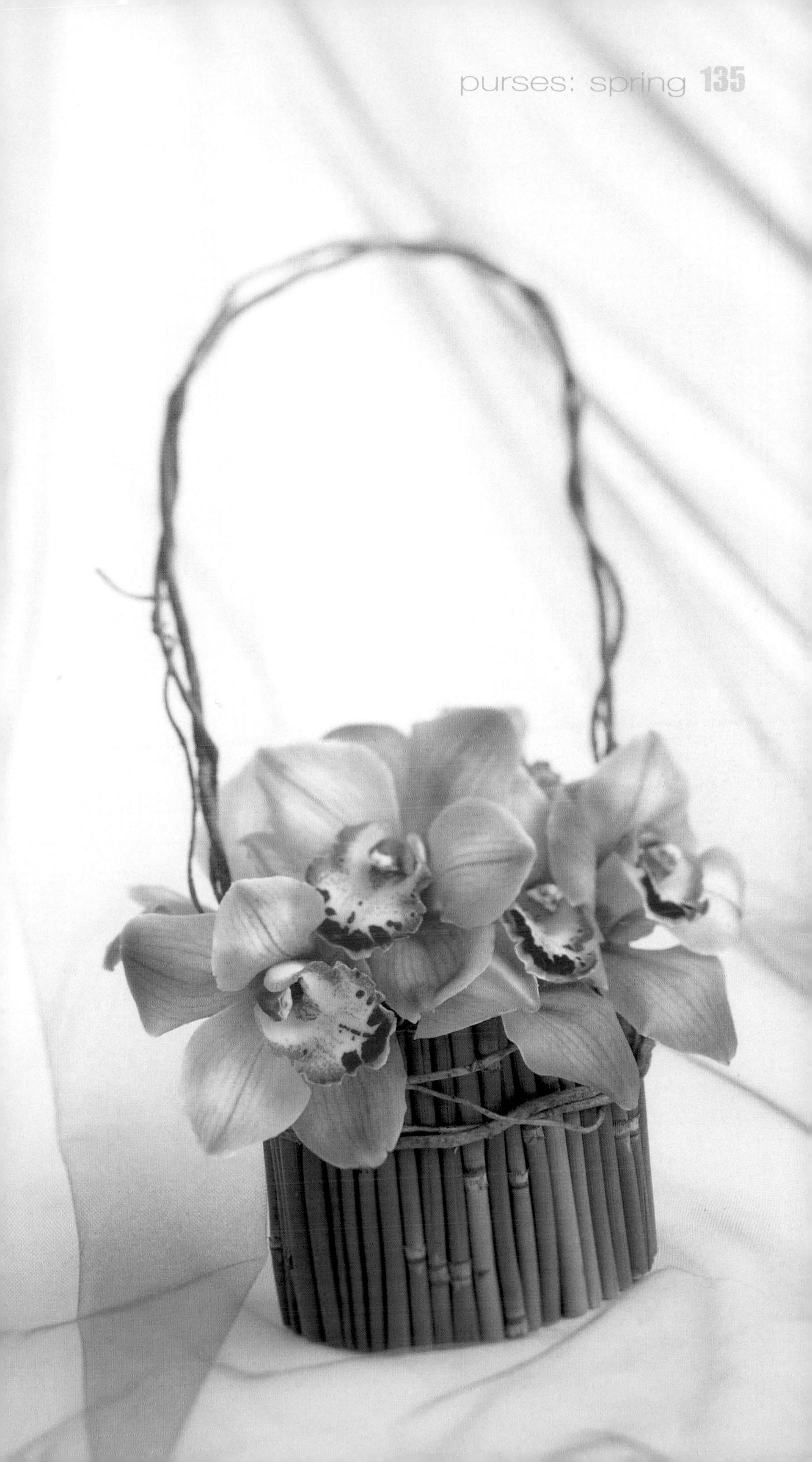

66

blooming bag

Florals take center stage in this leaf-covered purse bouquet.

1 Remove handles from the chip-wood basket. Lay ivy leaves face down, and spray them with adhesive.

2 Wait a few seconds until the adhesive becomes tacky. Apply the leaves to the box from the bottom up, overlapping them to fully cover the surface.

3 Apply a blade of lily grass to each side of the box with floral adhesive. Connect the two blades at the top with a small dab of adhesive to form the handle. Add plastic liner.

Any collection of summer blossoms would take center stage in this fabulous purse bouquet, which is arranged in a chip-wood basket that has been covered with ivy leaves. Here, *Calendula* and lavender are accented by blades of lily grass (*Liriope*). Two additional blades of lily grass form the handle.

Depending on the materials used, which could range from casual wildflowers to costly premium blooms, this versatile bridal accessory can be dressed up or down for daytime or evening celebrations. And the handsome ivy covering can be made a few days in advance, allowing last-minute assembly of the purse bouquet.

materials:

Calendula
lily grass (*Liriope*)
lavender
ivy leaves
chip-wood basket
plastic liner
Tack 1000 spray adhesive
Oasis Floral Adhesive

Pretty purses for the
bride and her maids.

1 Cut a rectangular piece of plastic foam, and glue it into the bottom of the purse.

2 Place florals into Aquapics. Apply a drop of glue to the end of each Aquapic, and insert each Aquapic into the foam.

3 Wire narrow black feathers into small bunches, and tuck them into the bouquet.

A modestly priced handbag, sold for about $20 at department stores, serves as the "holder" for this lush fall bouquet, which is composed of *Dahlias*, *Setaria* (millet), *Echinacea* (cone flower), and *Epidendrum* orchids.

Almost any similarly shaped purse can be adapted to hold wedding florals, as long as it flexes open cleanly with no flaps to obstruct the floral presentation. If well-chosen, the purses may also serve as gifts for the bridesmaids. And if desired by the bride, the wedding party may have a part in the purse selection, so the floral accessory is better planned and coordinated with the gowns.

materials:
Dahlias
Epidendrum orchids
millet (*Setaria*)
Echinacea
handbag
feathers
Aquapics
plastic foam
Oasis Floral Adhesive
wired picks

winter whites

1 Artfully wrap a papier-mâché cylinder with satin. Secure the fabric to the cylinder with corsage pins. To form the handle, pin both ends of a length of satin cording to the inside of the cylinder.

2 Glue a plastic liner to the inside of the cylinder. Glue a water-soaked Iglu Holder inside the liner. Top the cylinder's rim with a premade feather wreath; use corsage pins to hold the wreath in place.

3 Place three white roses into the foam cage. Attach Stay-Fresh Stephanotis Stems to the *Stephanotis* blossoms. Insert corsage pins into the flowers' centers, and place them into the design.

Elegantly clad in white satin, a papier-mâché cylinder, topped with a premade feather wreath, forms an exquisite purse bouquet. Premium florals and a satin-cording handle lend to the designs' sophisticated presentation.

Pearl-headed corsage pins, inserted into the centers of the delicate star-shaped *Stephanotis* blossoms, add a little shimmer and help make this creation ideal for brides planning wintertime or holiday season nuptials.

Fabric-covered boxes make coordinating colors easy. If desired, the fabric covering could even be the same as the wedding party's attire.

materials:

Stephanotis blossoms
roses
papier-mâché cylinder
feather wreath
satin fabric
satin cording
corsage pins
Stay-Fresh Stephanotis Stems
Oasis Iglu Holder
plastic liner
hot glue

In this noble scepter, the drama is in the details.

1 Use hot glue to secure a straight-handled bouquet holder inside a Lomey extender rod. Wrap the extender with double-stick tape, and wrap the tape-covered extender with white satin ribbon.

2 Affix the satin cording with floral adhesive, covering the entire extender rod and the base of the bouquet holder.

3 Wrap some of the roses with wide satin ribbon. Twist silver paddle wire around the base and the stem of each ribbon-covered rose, to hold the ribbon in place.

Comprising multicolor 'Peppermint' roses and dainty peach spray roses, this elegant bouquet, in grand scepter style, features an extra-long handle that has been accessorized with cording. The elongated handle is created with a Lomey extender into which a straight-handled bouquet holder has been secured.

Adding to the creation's regal appearance, loops of cording are woven throughout the floral placements, and tassels, attached to wood picks, are placed into the design. In addition, some of the standard roses are encased within loops of wide satin ribbon for a dramatic, hooded effect.

materials:

'Peppermint' roses
'Surprise' spray roses
cording
tassels
satin ribbon
Lomey extender
Wedding Belle Bouquet Holder
Oasis Floral Adhesive
hot glue
double-stick tape
silver paddle wire
wood picks

70 wired wheat

Fresh bearded wheat accents a summertime design.

Embellished with beading wire from top to bottom, fresh bearded wheat provides the support structure for this striking calla and yarrow scepter bouquet. The wheat, the lengthy stems of which serve as the bouquet's handle, is gathered into a haphazard bundle and holds a straight-handled bouquet holder. A wide banding of beading wire, just beneath the wheat heads, accents the stems and secures the bouquet holder in place.

Geranium foliage and bunches of pink yarrow are placed into the center of the bouquet holder while the trumpet-like calla blossoms are inserted around the perimeter with the help of floral adhesive.

1 Wrap the stems and heads of fresh bearded wheat with beading wire. Gather the wire-wrapped wheat into a bunch.

2 Secure a saturated bouquet holder into the center of the wheat bundle with hot glue. Just beneath the heads of wheat, wrap a wide band of beading wire.

3 Arrange yarrow and geranium foliage in the foam. Cut the calla stems short, and glue them into the bouquet holder—around the edge—with floral adhesive.

materials:
miniature callas
cottage yarrow
bearded wheat
geranium foliage
Wedding Belle Bouquet Holder
beading wire
hot glue
Oasis Floral Adhesive

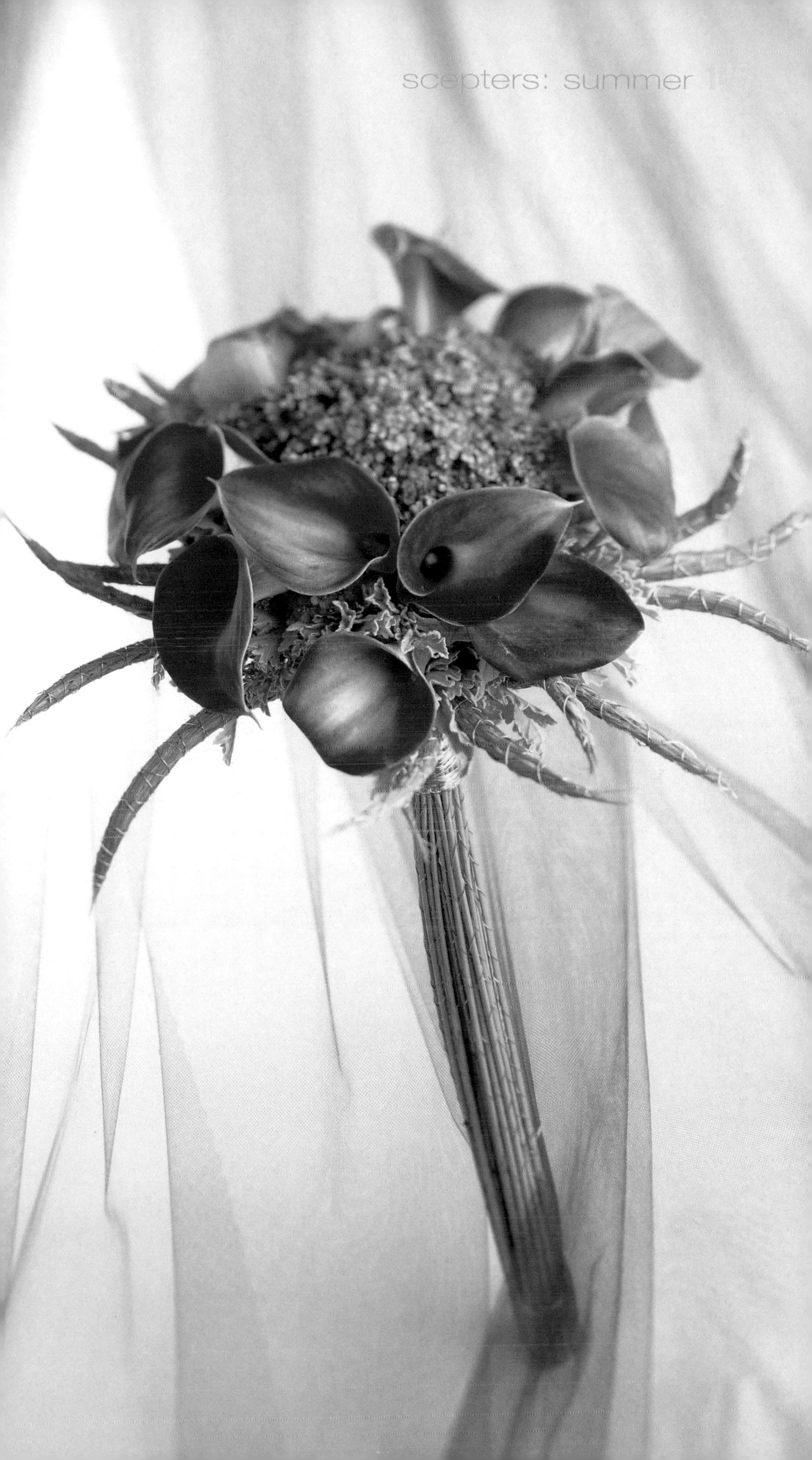

71 wand of roses

Truly a show stopper, this amazing floral scepter features a mound of sumptuous 'Moreno' roses atop a collar of millet (*Setaria*) and a texture-rich handle covered with barked wire and feathers.

The roses are arranged in a straight-handled bouquet holder, which is nestled into a banded bunch of millet. The millet stems, which form the scepter's handle, are then adorned with pheasant feathers, kept in place by a wrapping of beading wire. Coiled tightly around the handle, barked wire, along with feathers attached to beading wire, finish the handle with its angora-like texture.

1 Group two bunches of millet into a large bundle. Bind the grouping just beneath the heads with waterproof tape. Insert the straight-handled bouquet holder into the bundled millet.

2 Fill the bouquet holder with roses. Arrange them in a mounded fashion, allowing the millet to form an oversized collar around the flowers.

3 Place pheasant feathers onto the stems vertically, and wrap them with beading wire. Coil barked wire around the handle, and finish with a wrapping of beading wire to which small feathers are attached.

materials:

'Moreno' roses
millet (*Setaria*)
pheasant feathers and small feathers
Wedding Belle Bouquet Holder
beading wire
barked wire
Oasis waterproof tape

jewel of the Nile

Beaded ornaments glamorize a tropical blossom.

A fabulous 'Pink Ice' *Protea* is glamorously embellished with jeweled ornaments to create this exotic scepter bouquet. The bejeweled collar, fashioned from disassembled ornaments, as well as the dangling intact ornaments, adorn the unusual blossom for a fabulous black-tie affair.

The long *Protea* stem, wrapped with layers of ribbon and beading wire, is visually extended by the addition of another ornament at the end. Hot glue and beading wire will hold the stylish accessory in place for the duration of the event.

Inexpensive plastic ornaments are available from craft outlets during the Christmas season and work beautifully, both assembled and disassembled, for the wire-strung garlands that accent this tropical floral wand.

1 Remove the foliage from the stem of a 'Pink Ice' *Protea*. Wrap the stem with ribbon, and wrap the ribbon-covered stem with beading wire.

2 Disassemble several jeweled or beaded ornaments. String the individual jewels on beading wire. Wrap the strand of jewels around the base of the *Protea* blossom.

3 Attach two intact ornaments to ribbon, and allow them to dangle beneath the *Protea*. Glue a third ornament to the end of the *Protea* stem, and further adhere it to the stem with beading wire.

materials:
'Pink Ice' *Protea*
beaded ornaments
beading wire
hot glue

grass frame

A lily grass frame adds structure to a casual arrangement.

This attractive springtime sheaf, a monochromatic mixture of *Scabiosa*, blue lace flower, and rattail statice, arranged with a wildflower feel, is framed with long blades of lily grass. The lily grass, which is bent at the top and tucked into the design, adds a bit of structure to the flowers' somewhat unstructured appearance.

Although the taming effect of the lily grass framework lends a touch of formality to the composition, this loosely gathered bouquet is refreshingly casual and would serve beautifully at many types of events, particularly outdoor events, during the spring season.

1 Arrange flowers in a sheaf formation in one hand. With the other hand, bind the stems with waterproof tape.

2 Place blades of lily grass around the flowers. Bend the tips of the blades, and tuck them into the top portion of the bouquet. Bind them to the already bundled stems with waterproof tape.

3 Cover the waterproof tape with a blade of lily grass. Use boutonniere pins to attach it to the arrangement.

materials:

perennial *Scabiosa*
blue lace flower (*Didiscus*)
larkspur
rattail statice (*Limonium suworowii*)
lily grass (*Liriope*)
boutonniere pins
Oasis waterproof tape

summer blues

A lush arrangement for summertime celebrations.

1 Create the hand-tied arrangement, and bind the stems with waterproof tape. Tie a knot in each end of a wide piece of tulle.

2 Spread the tulle out, and hide the knotted ends by folding them back into the tulle. Fill the tulle pouch with rose petals.

3 Separate the petals into two groups inside the tulle, one in each end. Tie the petal-filled orbs around the flower stems.

Appropriate for practically any summertime wedding, this breathtaking monochromatic creation features gorgeous 'Pacific Giant' *Delphiniums* and delightfully fragrant 'Blue Bird' roses along with larkspur, *Phlox*, and fronds of sword fern (*Nephrolepis*).

To further distinguish this already magnificent bouquet, the sheaf is adorned not with a ribbon accent but with a pair of rose-petal-filled tulle "rosettes" that have been tied like a bow at the base of the floral materials. Once the petals dry, these orb accents can be used as sachets and offer a fragrant memento of the wedding day.

materials:

'Pacific Giant' *Delphinium*
'Blue Bird' roses
larkspur
Phlox
sword fern (*Nephrolepis*)
rose petals
tulle
Oasis waterproof tape

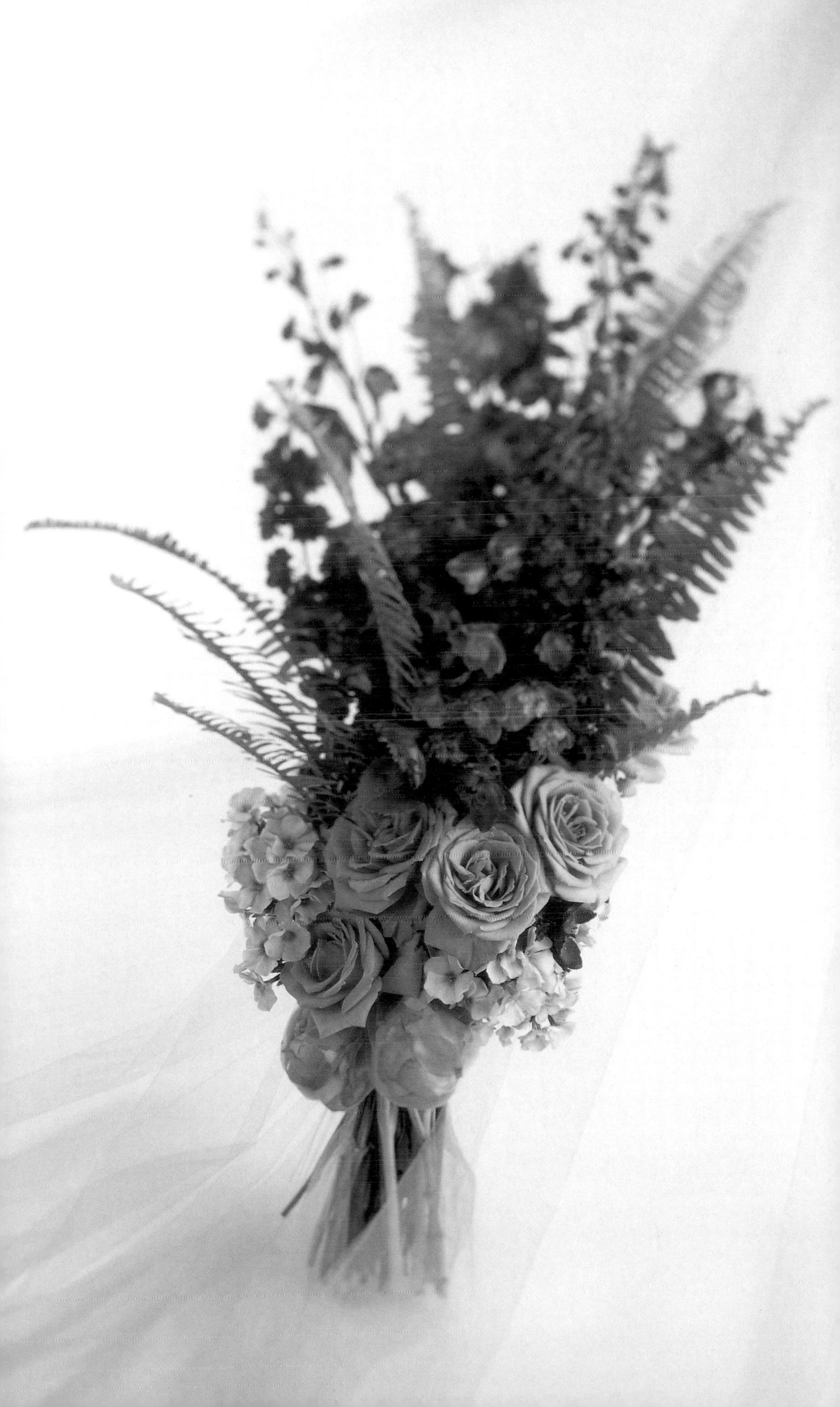

75

double binding

1 Arrange the floral materials in one hand; with the other hand, bind the stems with waterproof tape.

2 Slide two small craft store wreaths onto the tape-wrapped stems.

3 Twist raffia to create a "rope." Wrap it around the stems five times, and tie the ends in a knot to secure it in place.

Two wreaths and a raffia wrap band and bind the florals.

Glorious *Cymbidium* orchids are accented by an array of fall-colored materials in this fabulous autumnal bridal sheaf. Unusual foliages, such as *Grevillea* and 'Safari Sunset' *Leucadendron*, distinguish the creation and lend a subtly tropical feel to the mix.

Two miniature natural-vine wreaths bind the stems together and, along with a raffia twist, provide a natural slip-proof gripping point for brides and maids. With so many textures and colors, this sheaf will match almost any fall-toned gown and is ideal for today's modestly adorned bride and bridesmaid styles.

materials:

Cymbidium orchids
Dahlias
Sandersonia
Sedum
Pyracantha berries
Grevillea
'Safari Sunset' *Leucadendron*
two miniature wreaths
raffia
Oasis waterproof tape

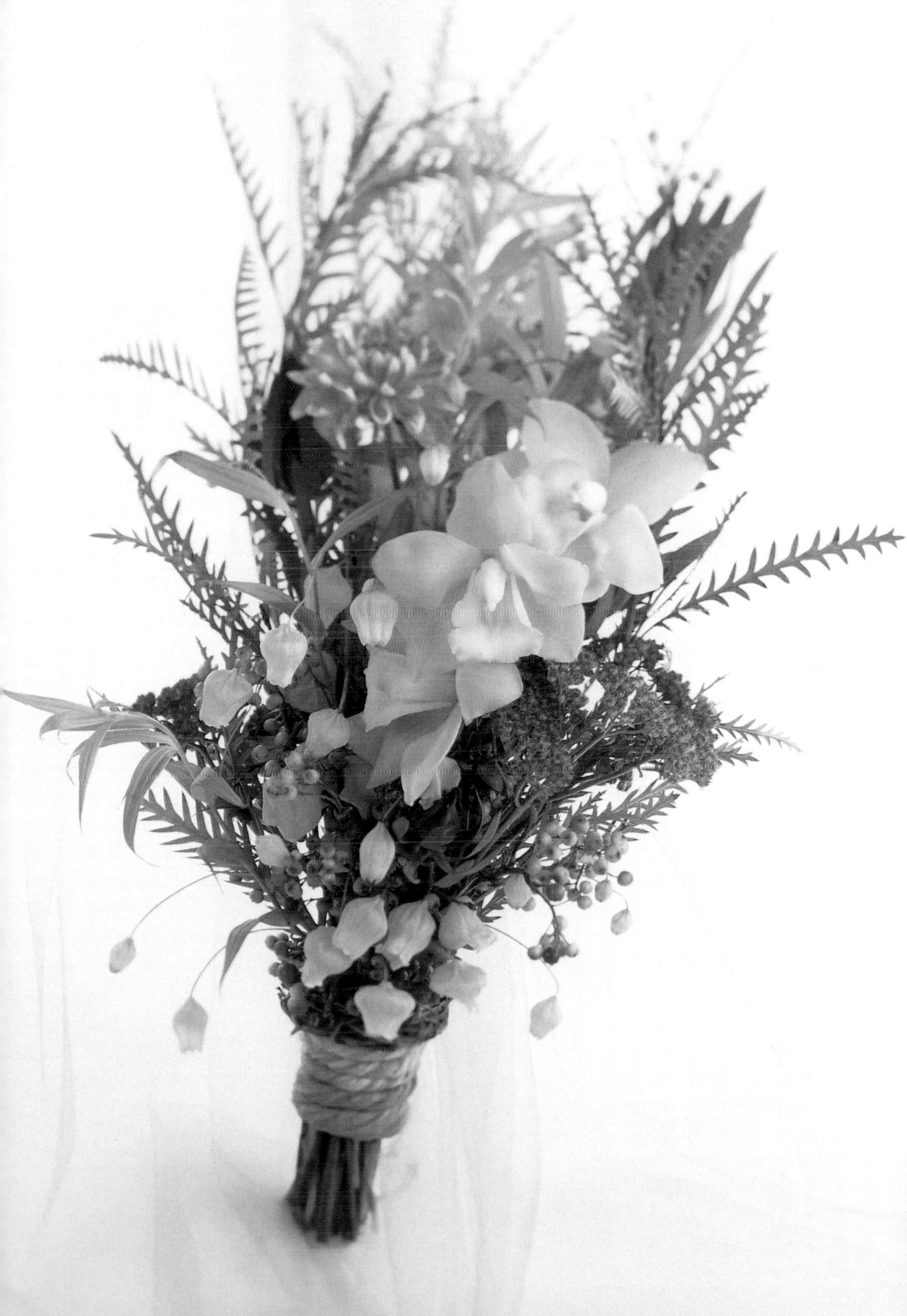

Layered ribbon applications finish this bouquet with holiday flair.

In the traditional colors of Christmas, this sumptuous arrangement is made even more luxurious by several wrappings of gold-edged, sheer red ribbon. The first treatment, covering several of the *Gerbera* stems, adds holiday sparkle into the depths of the design. After the flowers are arranged, the glitzy red ribbon is wrapped at the base of the bouquet, around the flowers' stems, and then twisted into cording and decoratively wrapped again.

Shiny glass-like permanent berries complete the traditional holiday presentation.

1 Wrap the *Gerbera's* stems with sheer red ribbon. Secure the ribbon at each end with floral adhesive.

2 Create a hand-tied arrangement, and bind the stems with waterproof tape. Wrap the grouped stems with the same sheer red ribbon.

3 Twist a length of the sheer red ribbon into "cording." Wrap the ribbon "cording" in a crisscross manner around the ribbon-wrapped stems.

materials:

'Ruby Red' roses
miniature *Gerberas*
Diosma folia
permanent berries
ribbon
Oasis waterproof tape
Oasis Floral Adhesive

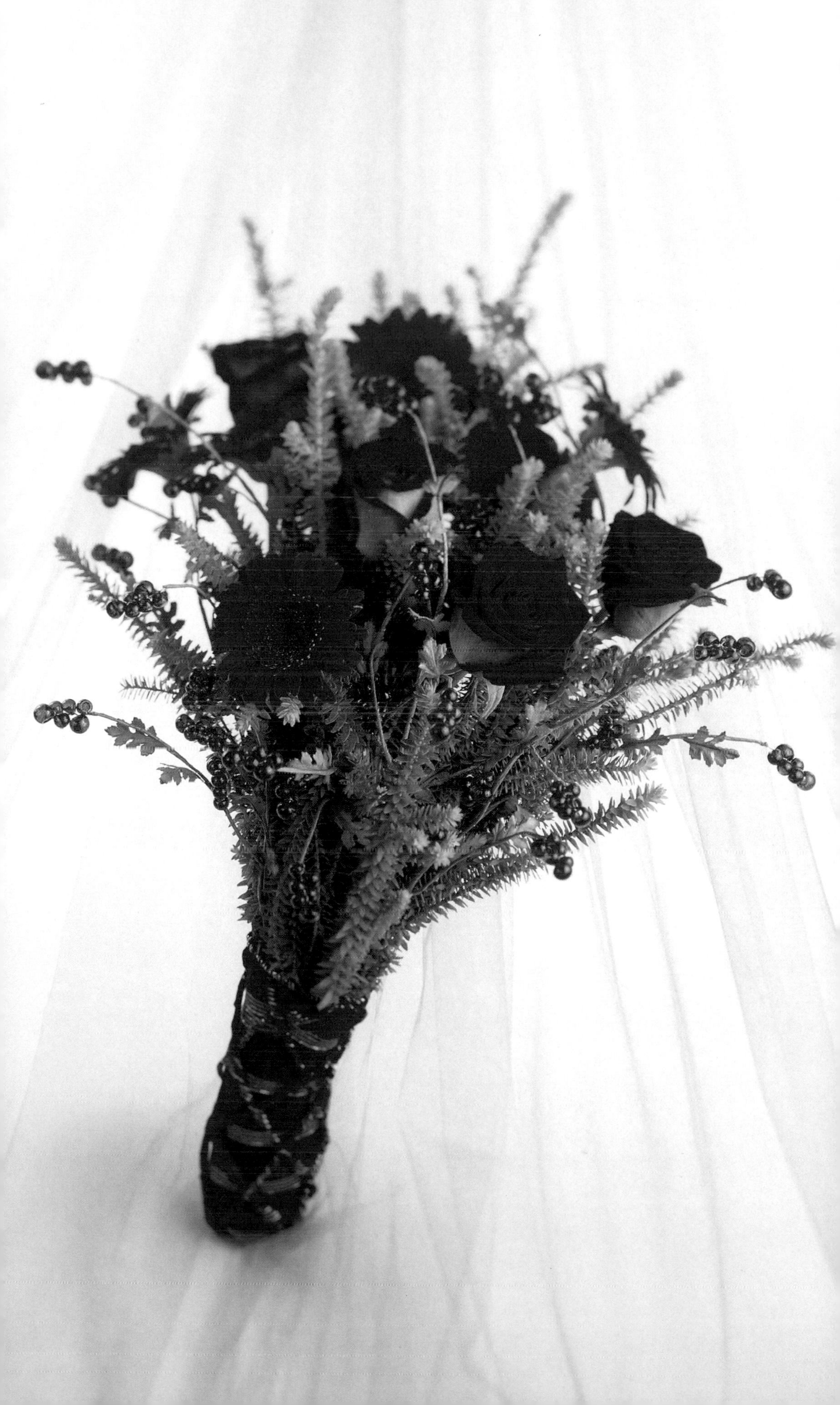

ring of ivy

Ivy vines support a profusion of spring florals.

1 Cover thin-gauge wire with brown floral tape. Strip the leaves from several ivy vines. Combine the vines into a wreath formation with the taped wire.

2 Add a few fully foliated ivy vines to the wreath. Leave long stems on the strands, so they may be combined with the florals.

3 Place flowers into the wreath form, so the blossoms rest on the vine structure. Gather the stems together, and bind them with waterproof tape. Cover the tape with a simple band of woven ribbon.

Featuring rich purples and pretty pinks, this lush, gardeny design will complement many spring color palettes. The fabulous flowers, which include lisianthuses, *Anemones*, heather, and *Spiraea*, are arranged in a wreath-like ring of ivy vines. The blossoms are simply tucked into the natural spaces formed between the vines. Once the flowers are arranged, more ivy is added in swirls that encircle the arrangement.

Such designs offer an economical advantage because they can do double duty at receptions. With the flowers' stems exposed, the bouquets can be dropped into vases placed on tables reserved for the bridal party.

materials:

Mariachi lisianthuses
Anemones
Scotch heather (*Erica melanthera*)
Spiraea
variegated ivy
ribbon
thin-gauge wire
brown floral tape
Oasis waterproof tape

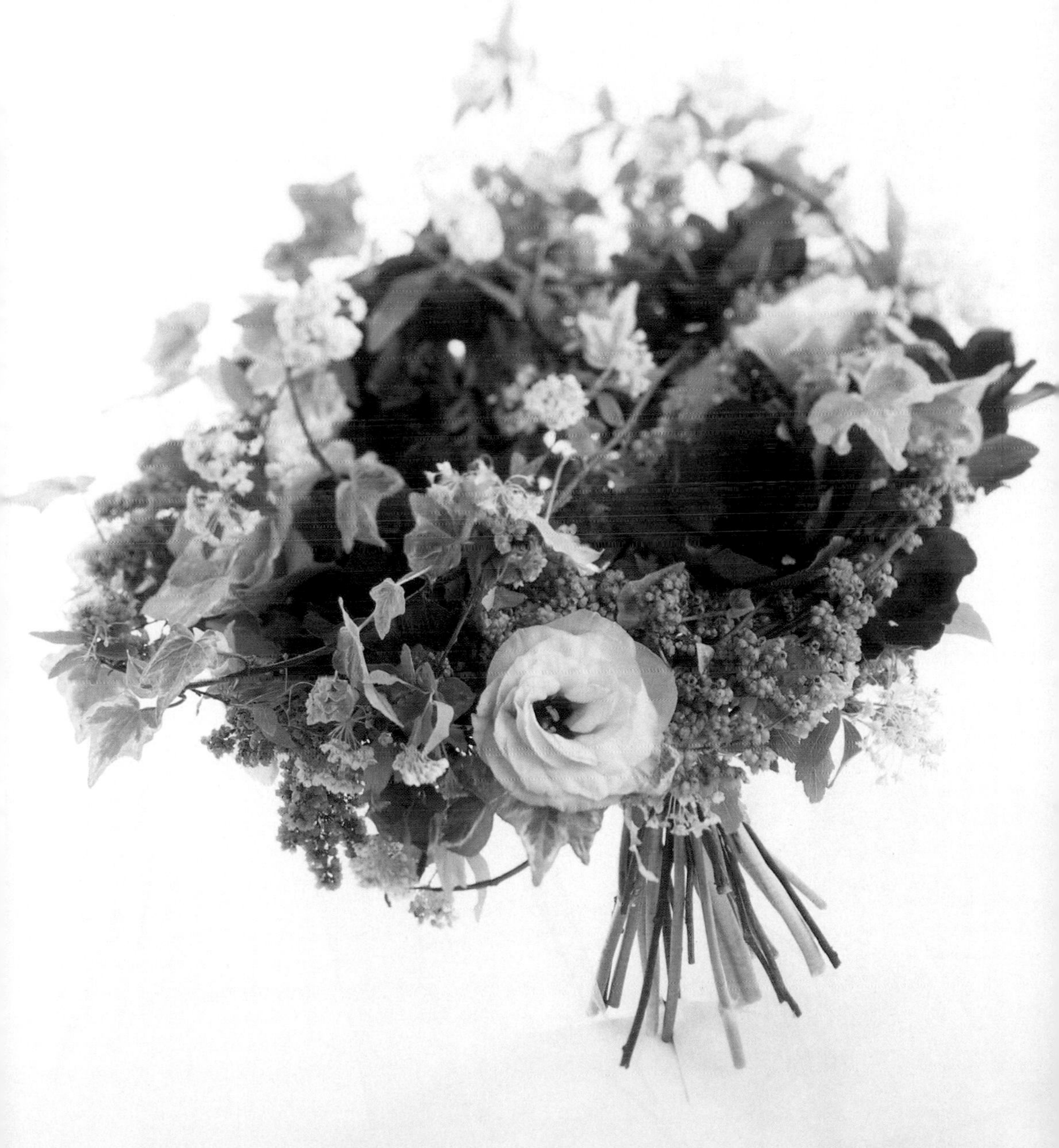

78

willow armature

An eye-catching horizontal crescent design for summer nuptials.

1 With beading wire, bind the ends of two long, arching curly willow branches to form an open crescent shape.

Formed of curly willow, an arching, crescent-shaped structure serves as a support mechanism for this summery mix of *Phlox*, roses, callas, and chinaberries. The curly willow armature, through which each stem is placed, elongates the rounded floral mass and makes the finished product appear to be an elevated crescent bouquet.

2 Bind short bits of curly willow perpendicularly to each long branch, filling in the open area between the two branches. Secure with beading wire.

Strands of lily grass, along with garlands of rolled rose petals and chinaberries strung on beading wire, are laced around and atop the floral arc and visually connect the blossoms to the curly willow armature to complete the summer creation.

3 Arrange the florals through the top of the crescent-shaped armature. Gather the stems together like a hand-tied bouquet, and bind them with waterproof tape. Cover the tape with ribbon.

materials:

'Charming Unique' roses
summer *Phlox*
miniature callas
lily grass (*Liriope*)
chinaberries
curly willow
ribbon
gold beading wire
Oasis waterproof tape

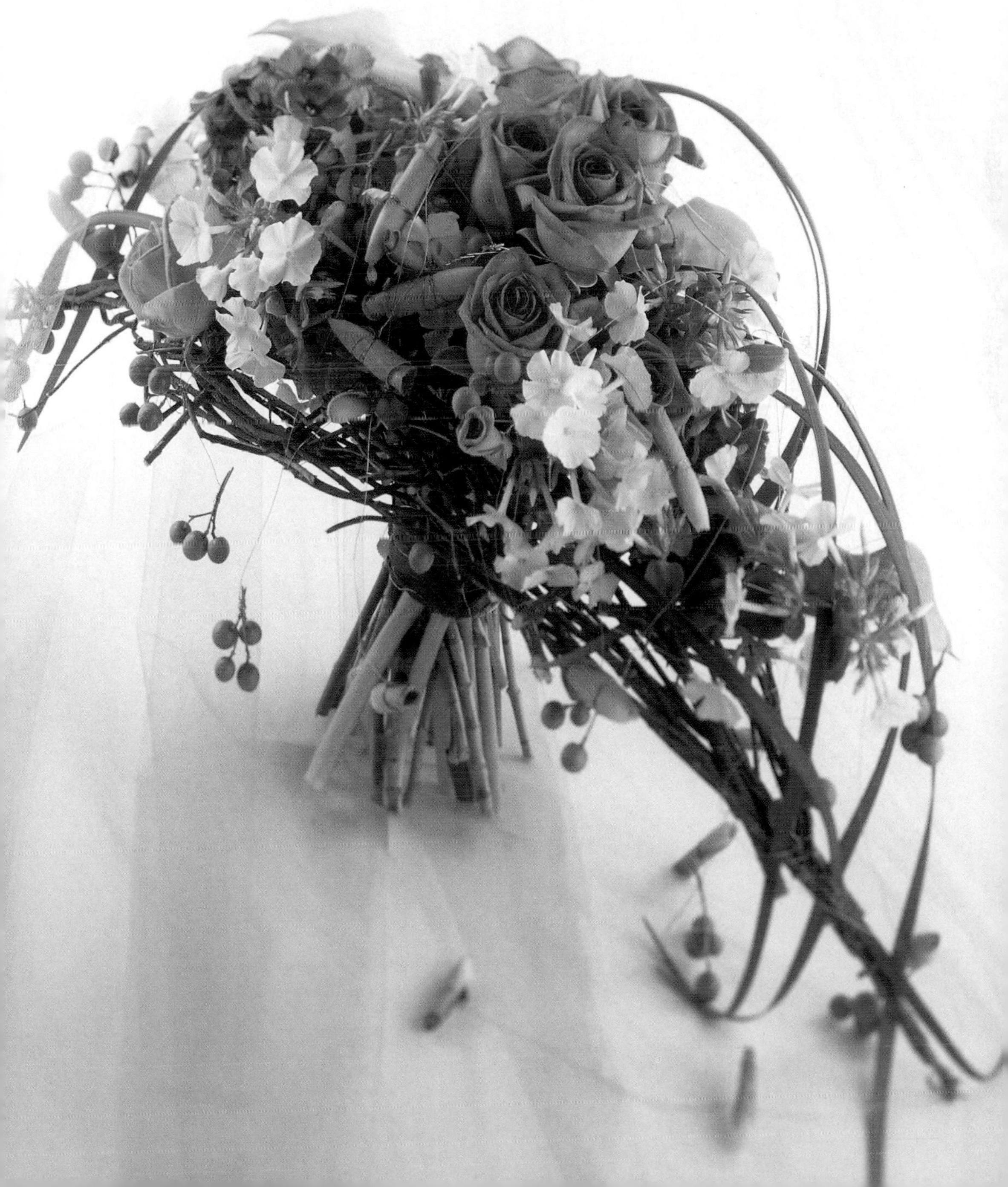

A V-shaped bouquet is backed by a curly willow structure.

1 With curly willow, create a V-shaped trellis-like support. Band the curly willow together with raffia.

2 Form a canoe-shaped bracing of curly willow bound with raffia. Use raffia to secure the bracing atop the willow "trellis."

3 Arrange flowers through the top of the structure, so the blossoms rest on its rim. Bind the stems to the structure with raffia.

A gathering of golden blossoms, accented by milkweed pods (*Asclepias*) and Queen Anne's lace, is arranged in a curly willow support structure. The bits of willow are bound together with raffia and form a V-shaped "trellis" that is topped with a horizontally placed, canoe-shaped bracing. The florals are placed into the bracing with some of the blossoms resting atop the rim. A garland of milkweed pods, strung on beading wire, also drapes the brace.

The design's form, materials, and bowing-head tulip placements give the composition a structured yet casual feel. Swirling twigs, tucked in and around the blooms, have a nature-made effect.

materials:

French tulips
miniature callas
Irises
Queen Anne's lace
milkweed pods (*Asclepias*)
curly willow
raffia
beading wire

Winter-white florals are arranged in a silver-painted twig ball.

1 Cut a hole into the bottom of a twig sphere. Spray the sphere with silver paint.

2 Insert florals into various openings in the sphere, and direct the stems through the newly cut hole.

3 Bind the stems with waterproof tape. Tie a bow from the satin ribbon. Secure the bow to the design with a corsage pin.

Supporting this elegant creation, composed of lilies, *Gerberas*, tulips, and stars of Bethlehem, is a loosely bound twig orb through which the florals are arranged. Although dropped into various openings, the stems protrude through a single hole that has been cut into the bottom of the orb.

Sprayed silver for a frosty effect, the armature, which is available in several different sizes to suit florals of various stem lengths, also serves as a decorative accent. A pretty bow, tied of premium satin ribbon, covers the binding and completes the wintry bouquet.

materials:

tulips
white 'Stargazer' lilies
Gerberas
stars of Bethlehem
twig orb
satin ribbon
Oasis waterproof tape
Super Silver spray paint
corsage pins

81 robin's nest

1 In the bottom of a premade nest, cut a hole big enough to accommodate the straight handle of a bouquet holder.

2 Drop the saturated bouquet holder into the opening in the nest. Cover the handle with brown florists' tape, and hot-glue the nest to the bouquet holder.

3 Wrap wired vines or other vining material around the bouquet holder's handle and around the base of the nest. Arrange flowers in the bouquet holder.

Bulb flowers and a bird's nest combine beautifully for spring.

Springtime treasures abound in this nature-inspired tussie-mussie, which is arranged in a straight-handled bouquet holder that has been dropped into the center of a pretty premade nest. To coordinate with the outdoorsy adornment, the bouquet holder's handle is covered with brown florists' tape and enwrapped with wired vines. Stem-wrapped florists' wire or leafless ivy vines could also be used to grace the bouquet holder's handle.

Once the handle and nest are accessorized with vining materials, luscious 'Eglantyne' garden roses and deliciously fragrant yellow *Freesia* are tightly placed in a well-ordered fashion.

materials:

'Eglantyne' garden roses
Freesias
wired vines or other vining material
premade nest
Wedding Belle Bouquet Holder
brown florists' tape
hot glue

1 Spray the back-sides of fresh ivy leaves with adhesive. Apply the leaves to the base and handle of a straight-handled bouquet holder.

2 Place geranium leaves into the bouquet holder to form an edging. Cut flower stems short, and arrange the flowers in a tight grouping.

3 Tie a bow, and knot each streamer. Add the knotted bow into the design.

Small, compact designs serve a variety of summer needs.

It is often said that good things come in small packages. And for summer brides, that sentiment aptly describes this tightly arranged, monochromatic mixture of tender blossoms. It's an ideal accessory, and depending on the florals selected, such tussie-mussies can be equally appropriate for both day and evening nuptials.

Adding to its elegance and distinction, this uncontrived offering is arranged in a bouquet holder that has been covered with ivy leaves. The leaf-covered handle is further adorned with a pretty tie of premium white ribbon.

materials:

roses
miniature *Gerberas*
Phlox
Bouvardia
Amaranthus
Queen Anne's lace
lisianthuses
scented geranium leaves
variegated ivy
ribbon
Wedding Belle Bouquet Holder
Tack 1000 spray adhesive

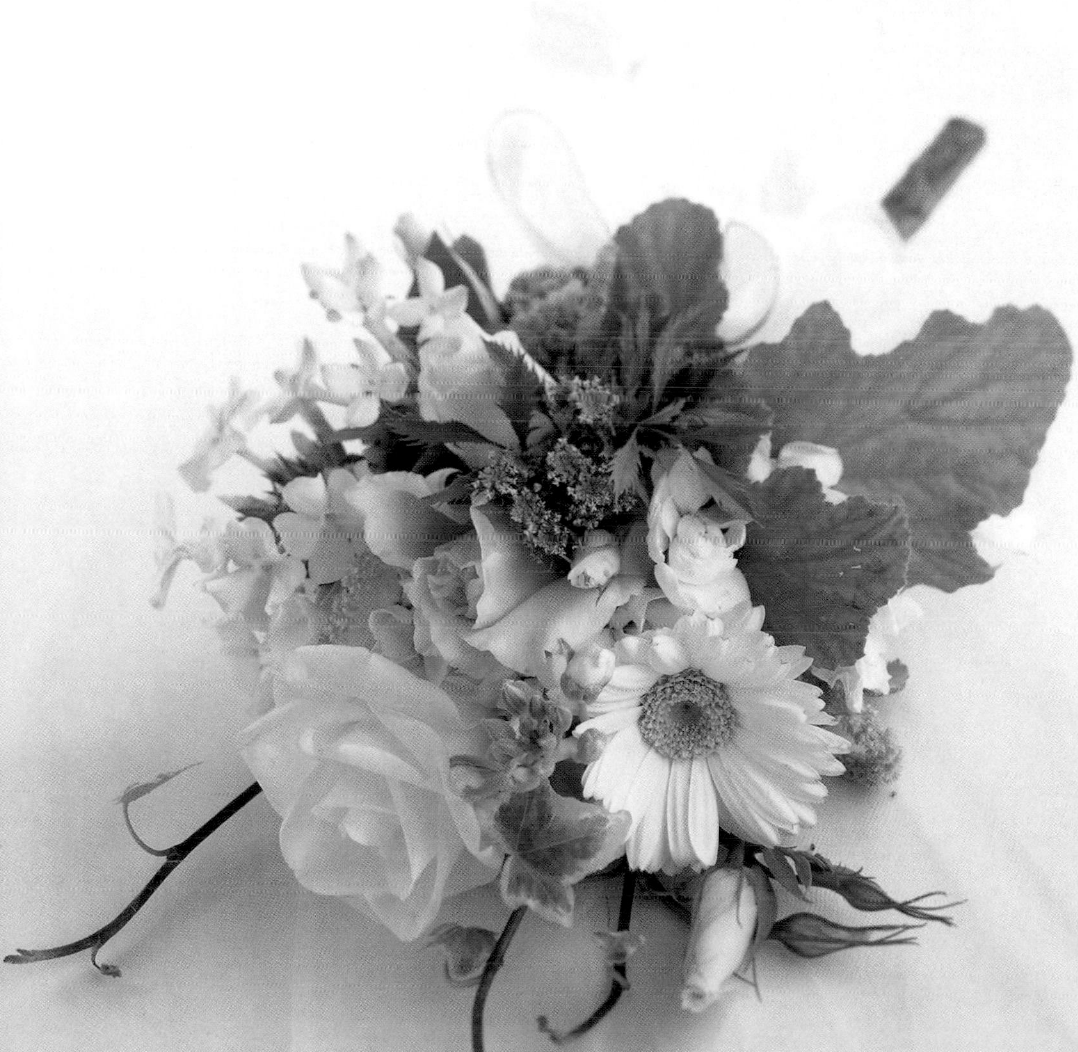

83 doily basket

Dip a crocheted doily into a fabric stiffener solution. Wring out the doily to remove excess liquid.

2 Place the doily onto a straight-handled bouquet holder, and allow it to dry for 24 hours. As it begins to dry, gently shape the edges for a scalloped look. Once it's dry, remove the doily from the bouquet holder, and saturate the foam.

3 Replace the doily on the holder. Slip leaves between the doily and the foam, so the foam is concealed. Arrange florals. Cover the bouquet holder's handle with a wrap of velvet ribbon, and finish with a bow.

Fall flowers are showcased in a doily-covered holder.

A charming fall bouquet, comprising roses, chrysanthemums, *Gerberas* (with the petals removed), stock, and variegated buckthorn (*Rhamnus*), is created using a dainty crocheted doily. Immersed in a fabric-stiffening solution, the doily is lightly shaped with a scalloped edge.

Enwrapping a bouquet holder, the doily forms a basket-like container that appears to hold the collection of blossoms, which are actually arranged in the bouquet holder's foam. Because the doily's loose crochet pattern would allow the bouquet holder to be visible, leaves, saved from the roses or other blossoms, are tucked between the doily and the bouquet holder, to conceal the mechanics.

materials:
roses
chrysanthemums
stock
Gerberas
variegated buckthorn (*Rhamnus*)
saved leaves
velvet ribbon
crocheted doily
Stiffy Fabric Stiffener
Wedding Belle Bouquet Holder

84 Christmas bells

Arranged in a bell, this design epitomizes the spirit of the season.

1. Apply duct tape to the inside of the cup of a brass bell. Hot-glue a saturated foam cage into the tape-covered cup.

2. Arrange the floral materials, including the leafless rose calyxes, in the cage.

3. Gather and periodically knot the ribbon. Tie the knotted ribbon into a bow, and insert the bow into the arrangement.

Rich, velvety red roses take center stage in this Christmas-inspired arrangement. In concert with the holiday feel, the materials, which also include *Hypericum* berries, cockscomb (*Celosia*), geranium leaves, and rosemary, are arranged in a foam cage that has been glued to the cup of a brass bell. Blemished or imperfect roses, whose petals have been removed, are wonderful additions—their colors and star-like calyx formations add garden-gathered sophistication.

Sheer burgundy ribbon, knotted periodically and tied into a bow, accessorizes the tussie-mussie and its pretty brass bell.

materials:

roses
Hypericum berries
cockscomb (*Celosia*)
rosemary
lemon-scented geranium leaves
brass bell
burgundy ribbon
Aquafoam cage
duct tape
hot glue

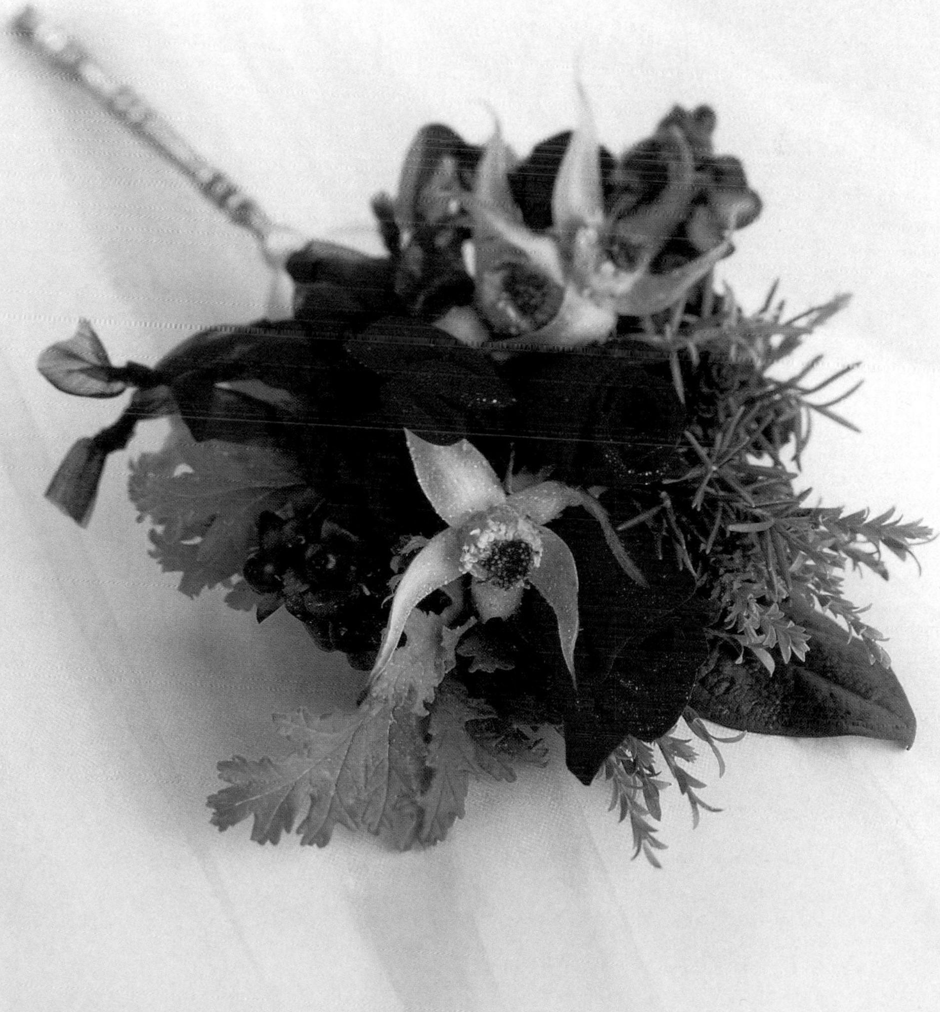

natural canopy

1 Cover the base of the foam with heather in a radiating formation that outlines the bouquet.

The gossamer fronds of wedding fern veil this spring design.

Known commonly as wedding fern, *Asparagus plumosus* is ideal for use in wedding bouquets. Here, the delicate fern, added as a finishing touch, forms a striking natural canopy over this incredible composition of spring blossoms.

The monochromatic collection, which should be pleasingly fragrant, includes heather, hyacinths, tulips, *Freesias*, and waxflower. The bouquet's shape, as well as its gossamery fern covering, which appears to hover above the bouquet, lend themselves to spring's more formal affairs.

2 Tuck the other florals into the foam between the bits of heather. Tape chenille stems to any stem that seems too delicate for foam insertion.

3 Insert the wedding fern so that it cascades over the bouquet—down the back and the sides, forming a natural veil.

materials:

Scotch heather (*Erica melanthera*)
hyacinths
tulips
waxflower
Freesias
wedding fern (*Asparagus plumosus*)
Wedding Belle Bouquet Holder
chenille stems
floral tape

A lily grass veil and leaf-covered stems enhance this bouquet.

1 Hand-tie roses in a round, slightly mounded formation. Bind the roses' stems with waterproof tape.

2 Create the veiling with a series of lily grass loops. Bind the lily grass to the roses with another wrapping of waterproof tape.

3 Spray the back-side of a variegated *Aspidistra* leaf with adhesive. Once the adhesive is tacky, wrap the roses' stems with the leaf.

Arching blades of lily grass envelop these roses in a sensation of swirls and loops, resulting in a distinctive bouquet for brides and maids. While the eye-catching veiling sets this design apart, its finishing touch, a large *Aspidistra* leaf that is wrapped around the roses' stems, completes the presentation with style.

The variegated leaf, chosen to match the intriguing color patterns of the unusual 'Peppermint' roses, is sprayed with adhesive and neatly adheres to the rose stems. The two all-natural, botanical-craft treatments add a bit of formality to the creation, enabling its use at both formal and semi-formal celebrations.

materials:
'Peppermint' roses
lily grass (*Liriope*)
variegated *Aspidistra*
Tack 2000
Oasis waterproof tape

wire cocoon

Gold beading wire envelops a plethora of fall florals.

Gold beading wire forms a cocoon-like covering for this incredible massing of autumnal flowers. Much of the beading wire, which is attached to picks in short sprays, is concentrated around the bouquet's edge while additional wire is wrapped across the center to finish the veiling effect.

From unopened buds to petal-dropped heads, the floral materials include blossoms at several stages of life. *Dahlias*, for example, range from bud to full bloom to heads without petals, and carnations are featured in full bloom as well as blossomless calyxes. Other featured materials include sunflowers, *Sedum*, and *Hypericum* berries.

1 Arrange the botanicals in a bouquet holder, using buds as well as fully open flowers for a varied look.

2 Attach several pieces of beading wire to wood picks. Curve the wires into arching sprays. Insert the picks into the foam around the bouquet's edge.

3 Wrap additional beading wire to form the cocoon-like covering that starts at the edge of the bouquet and covers the center.

materials:

carnations
Dahlias
'Indian Summer' sunflowers
Sedum
Hypericum berries
bouquet holder
beading wire
wood picks

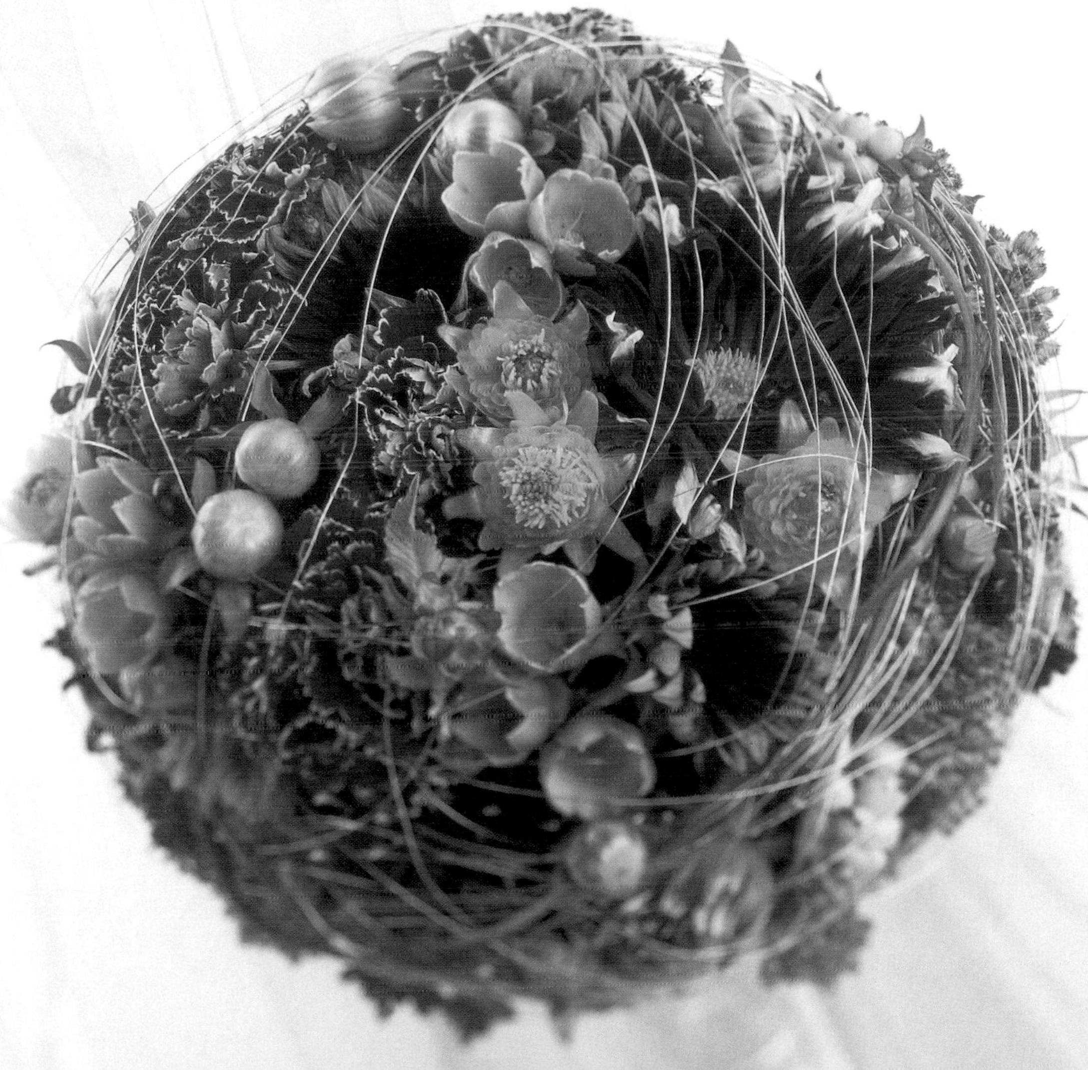

wedding veil

Covered with tulle veiling, this bouquet is a natural for the bride.

1 Hand-tie the roses in a mounded, cone-shaped formation. Bind the stems with waterproof tape.

2 Cover the roses with tulle, and gather the fabric at the base of the flowers, binding it with another wrapping of tape. Cut the tulle from the bolt, and make sure the length exceeds that of the rose stems.

3 Pin the tulle into the bottoms of the roses' stems with corsage pins, completely covering the cut ends.

Echoing the covering traditionally worn by the bride, this pretty mound of roses, comprising 'Akita' and fragrant 'Blue Bird' varieties, is shrouded in silvery sheer tulle. The roses are arranged in a tall mound—almost a cone—and the tulle is simply draped over the mound and attached at the bottom with corsage pins.

Feminine and delicate, it's a natural to be carried by the bride, but this veiling treatment could be applied to bridesmaids' flowers as well. And if their gowns are light in color, the tulle fabric could be selected to match the gowns.

materials:

'Akita' roses
'Blue Bird' roses
tulle
corsage pins
Oasis waterproof tape

89 ribbon base

Gorgeous spring blossoms are glued into a multilooped bow.

1 Tie several six-loop bows of various blue and purple ribbons.

2 Combine the bows together to form a mound. Secure the grouping with medium-gauge wire, leaving a wire "stem."

3 Fill the cup of the tussie-mussie with plastic foam, and insert the wire "stem." Dip the flowers' stems into floral adhesive, and tuck them into the ribbon.

Placed amid the loops of an oversized bow, which has been tied to form a beribboned mound, these pretty pastel and burgundy florals form a dainty posy style bouquet. A Victorian-inspired tussie-mussie, filled with foam, holds the multilooped bow.

To create the bouquet, the fresh cut flowers are dipped into floral adhesive and tucked between the ribbon loops. The adhesive will help keep the flowers hydrated, but such a design is best if created at the last minute. The ribbon base can be assembled in advance, and gluing in the florals will be a quick job.

materials:
roses
'Atilla' tulips
Mariachi lisianthuses
Irises
ribbon
tussie-mussie
Oasis Floral Adhesive
plastic foam
medium-gauge wire

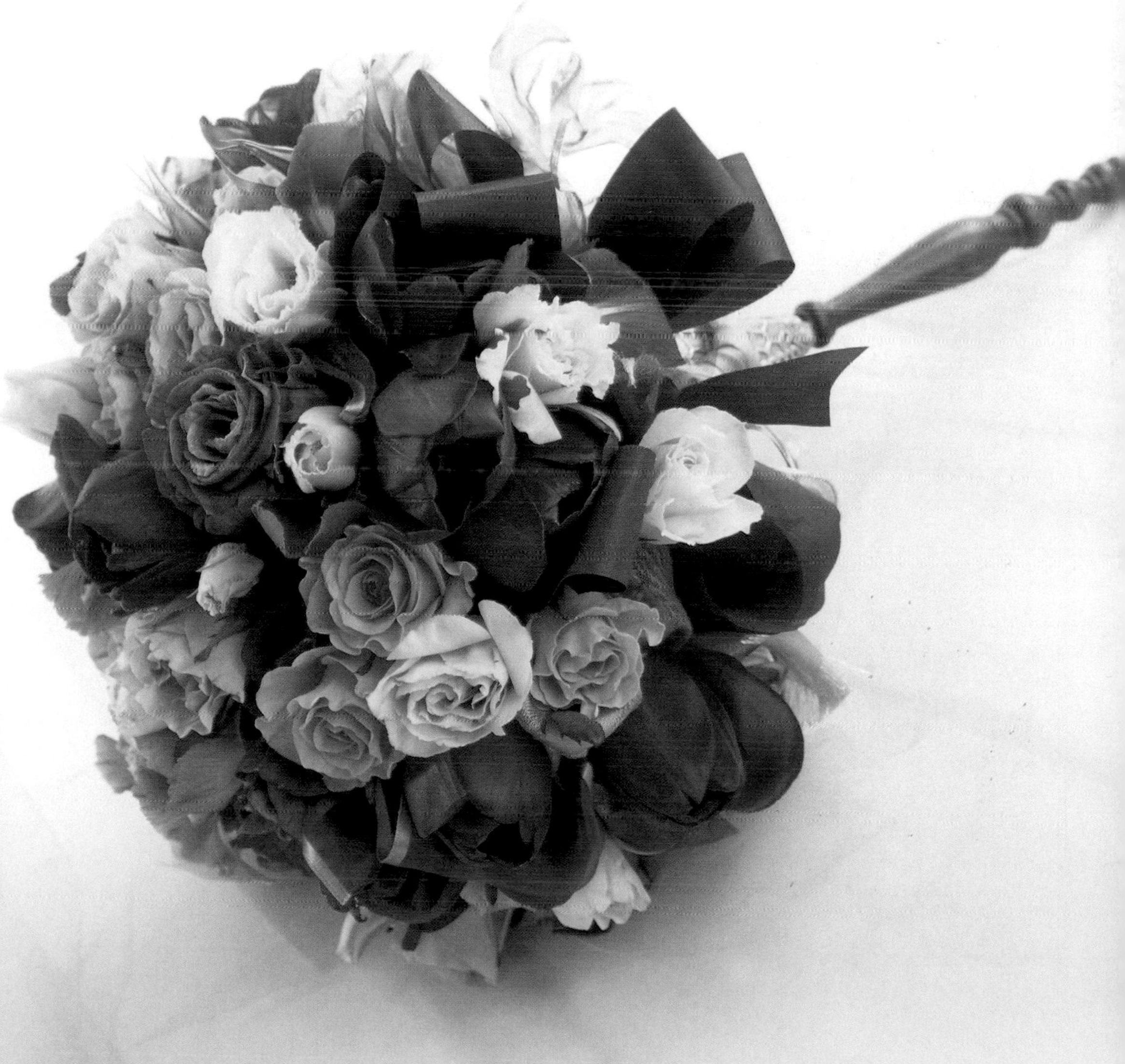

90 pearled posy

A petite Victorian-style bouquet holder makes a grand statement.

1 Cut the tip off of a foam cone. Spray adhesive to the back-sides of *Eucalyptus* leaves. Apply the leaves to the foam cone in an overlapping manner until the cone is completely covered.

2 Hot-glue a resin tussie-mussie to the narrow end of the leaf-covered cone. Spray a strand of faux pearls with English Gray paint. Pin the painted pearls to the foam cone, just above the tussie-mussie.

3 Hot-glue a saturated foam cage atop the broad end of the leaf-covered cone. Arrange florals in the foam cage.

This romantic bouquet, featuring a pretty collection of lavender and blue florals, is created in a foam cage that rests atop a leaf-covered cone. An ornately detailed resin tussie-mussie, glued to one end of the cone, highlights the breathtaking composition and is accessorized by a strand of pearls painted to match the tiny Victorian-style bouquet holder.

Clearly Victorian in its shape, color, and styling, this elegant bouquet is true to its heritage. And like the posies of Queen Victoria's era, this one could be carried by brides and maids alike at nearly any type of summer ceremony.

materials:

Delphinium
silver *Brunia*
seeded *Eucalyptus*
Eucalyptus leaves
sea holly
plastic foam cone
faux pearls
English Gray paint
Tack 2000 spray adhesive
tussie-mussie
Aquafoam cage
hot glue
boutonniere pins

91 ribbon updates

Modern-day ribbon treatments for an old-fashioned posy.

1 With floral stem wrap, secure two lengths of heavy-gauge wire to the handle of a Designette.

2 Bind a group of *Gerbera* stems, near the base and top, with waterproof tape. Insert the wire-handled Designette into the *Gerbera* stem bunch.

During the early years of Queen Victoria's reign, flowing ribbons, particularly those in pastel hues, characterized the bouquets. In that royal tradition, this gracious gathering of roses, *Gerberas*, *Hypericum* berries, and more is accented by long streamers of sheer ribbon.

In a new twist on Victorian accents, the bouquet's handle—stem-covered heavy-gauge wires taped to the end of a Designette—features a modern-day ribbon treatment. Short strands of sheer, fall-hued ribbon are wrapped around the stem-covered handle and tied into knots. The loose ends of the ribbons are then trimmed into short tufts for a striking beribboned presentation.

3 Wrap short lengths of sheer ribbon once around the *Gerbera* stems, and tie them into knots. Clip the loose ends short. Arrange florals. Tie a bow with long streamers, and add it to the bouquet.

materials:

roses
miniature *Gerberas*
Hypericum berries
Trachelium
millet (*Setaria*)
Designette Floral Design Tool
sheer ribbon
heavy-gauge wire
floral stem wrap
Oasis waterproof tape

two hearts

Crocheted hearts lend Victorian charm to a simple design.

1 Arrange roses and *Camellia* foliage in a bouquet holder. Apply spray adhesive to the back-sides of *Galax* leaves, and affix the leaves to the back of the bouquet holder.

2 Insert a hairpin-shaped wire into a crocheted lace heart. Insert the heart into the foam of the bouquet holder.

3 Gather the heart-shaped doily like a handkerchief. Wrap the corner with floral tape, so the doily won't wick moisture from the flowers. Insert the taped doily into the foam.

Pretty 'Charming Unique' roses, along with *Camellia* leaf accents, compose this elegant design, which is accessorized by a three-dimensional crocheted lace heart. Replacing the traditional bow, a crocheted heart-shaped doily cascades from the base of the floral cluster.

With a modest use of florals, as is typical of Victorian posies, a few additional elements will help disguise the bouquet holder and yield a polished presentation. Here, *Galax* leaves, sprayed with adhesive, are applied to the back-side of the bouquet holder to decoratively conceal the white plastic base.

materials:

'Charming Unique' roses
Camellia leaves
Galax leaves
lace heart
heart-shaped doily
floral tape
medium-gauge wire
Tack 2000 spray adhesive
Bouquet Mates bouquet holder

fresh cuttings

1 Spray the back-sides of fresh ivy leaves with adhesive.

2 Apply the leaves to a square of fabric, starting at the edges and working inward. Overlap the leaves so no fabric is visible.

3 Arrange the tulips. Bind the grouping with waterproof tape. Wrap the tulips with the leaf-covered fabric, and finish with a band of coordinating ribbon.

Ivy-covered fabric enwraps a bundle of spring's finest tulips.

Like a newly purchased bunch of tissue-wrapped fresh cut tulips, this pretty spring bouquet is bundled into a leaf-covered square of facing fabric. Several varieties of pastel-colored tulips, which are bound with waterproof tape and then wrapped in the leaf-covered fabric, compose the bouquet. A band of coordinating ribbon enwraps the group and completes the design. Although the florals are simply bunched and banded, the ivy wrapping dresses up the design for practically any kind of nuptial celebration.

For a faster version of this technique, apply *Galax* leaves, rather than ivy, to the fabric. Because the leaves are larger than most ivy varieties, *Galax* will cover the space more quickly.

materials:

French tulips
variegated ivy leaves
facing fabric
ribbon
Tack 1000 spray adhesive
Oasis waterproof tape

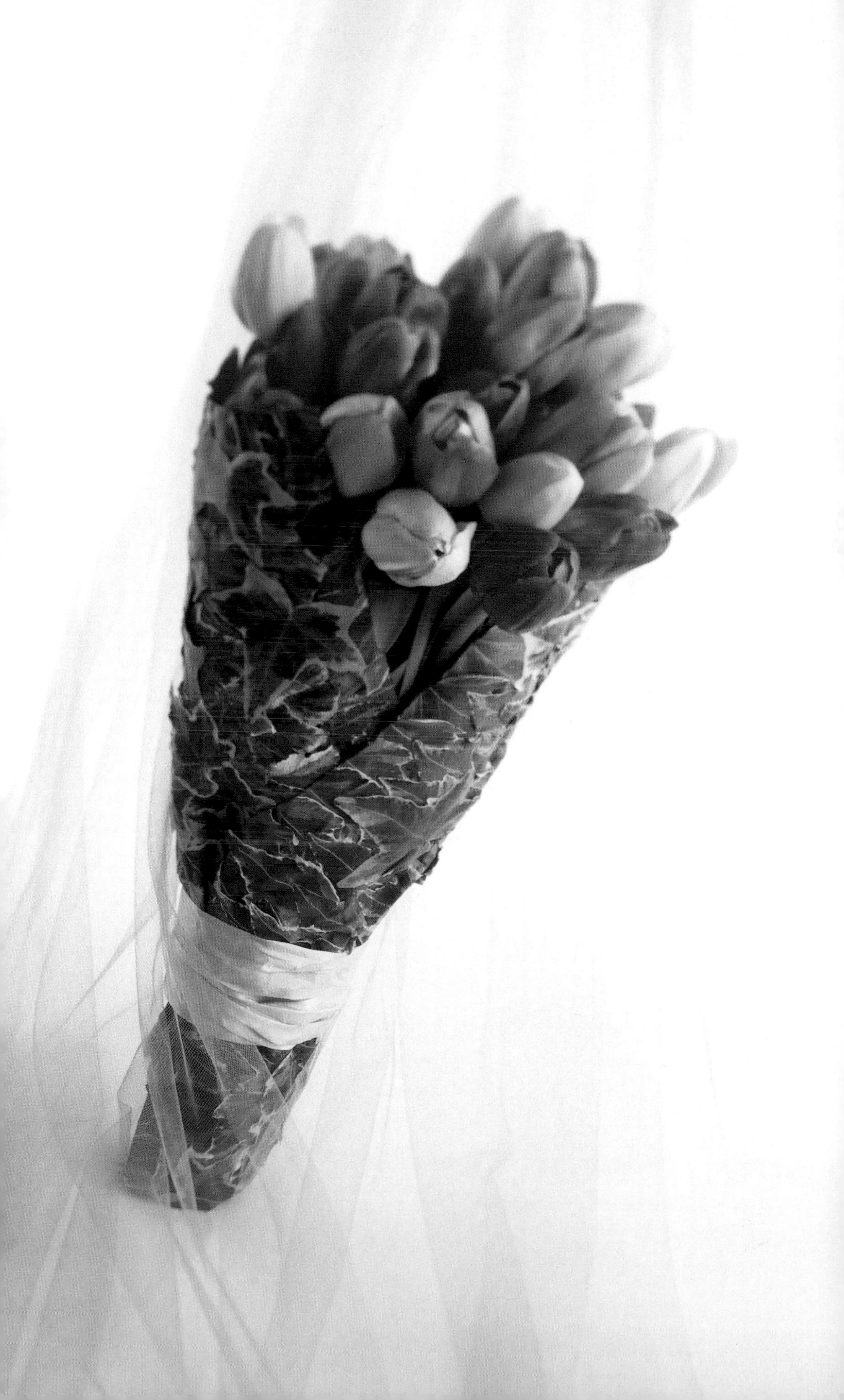

Variegated ginger
leaves envelop a
sheaf-like design.

1 Arrange callas. Surround the blossoms with vertically placed ginger leaves. Bind with waterproof tape.

Taken from exotic ginger plants, several broad glossy leaves gracefully envelop a sunny collection of miniature callas. The yellowish variegation of the ginger-leaf wrapping coordinates beautifully with the yellow callas and enhances the bouquet's dignified appearance. But if the bride prefers something other than yellow, miniature callas offer a multitude of color choices, many of which would be complemented by the ginger leaves.

Regal enough for the bride and easy enough to be made in multiples for attendants, this sleek sheaf-like creation has an air of formality that dictates its use at grand summertime events.

2 Make the remaining leaves (two or three) more pliable by cutting away some of their apexes.

3 Spray the back-sides of the leaves with adhesive. Starting just below the blossoms, wrap the design with the leaves.

materials:
miniature callas
variegated ginger leaves
Tack 2000 spray adhesive
Oasis waterproof tape

95 fabric cloak

1 Snip off half of the handle of a straight-handled bouquet holder. With hot glue, secure the bouquet holder into a plastic foam cone.

2 Arrange the flowers in the bouquet holder. Double the fabric over, and tape the two loose ends together with double-stick tape. Lay the bouquet into the fabric, and wrap the bouquet.

3 At the base of the bouquet holder, tape the fabric to cinch it around the flowers. Cover the tape with a band of ribbon.

Textured fabric wraps a fabulous fall arrangement.

Encircling a lush arrangement of roses, *Dahlias*, cockscomb, and more, a double layer of textured fabric forms a cloak for the russet-toned gathering, which is arranged in a large straight-handled bouquet holder.

Dimension is added to the handle of the bouquet holder, which is snipped short, by hot-gluing it into a plastic foam cone, enabling the fabric to drape nicely and providing an easy-grip handle. The fabric is cinched at the base of the flowers with tape, and a band of ribbon conceals the tape.

materials:

'Hocus Pocus' standard roses
'The Prince' garden roses
Dahlias
Hypericum berries
annual *Scabiosa*
Amaranthus
Wedding Belle Bouquet Holder
ribbon
textured fabric
gold bullion
plastic foam cone
Oasis waterproof tape
hot glue
double-stick tape

Winter white trappings for elegant cool-weather nuptials.

1 Cut a cardboard disk approximately 8 to 10 inches in diameter. Cut a hole, approximately two inches in diameter, in the center of the disk.

2 Insert the pleated silk fabric, gathered into a "tube," into the center of the cardboard disk. Spread the fabric to cover the disk, and gather the ends underneath it, so the fabric drapes the disk.

3 Top the cardboard disk with a premade feather wreath. Drop the bouquet into the center of the wreath and disk. Wrap the ribbon drape and the stems with waterproof tape. Cover the tape with ribbon.

Dressed in cool weather attire, this winter white nosegay, composed of *Nerines*, spray roses, and artificial white raspberries, is enwrapped with a feather wreath and pleated silk ribbon, which covers a large cardboard disk.

Suitable for both brides and bridesmaids, this bouquet, and its elegant wrap treatment, are easy and quick to make. The feather wreath is purchased premade, and cutting and wrapping the cardboard disk takes just a few minutes. The hand-tied nosegay, in which each blossom is wired and taped, is simply dropped into a hole that has been cut in the center of the disk.

materials:

Nerines
spray roses
artificial white raspberries
premade feather wreath
pleated silk fabric
ribbon
cardboard disk
Oasis waterproof tape

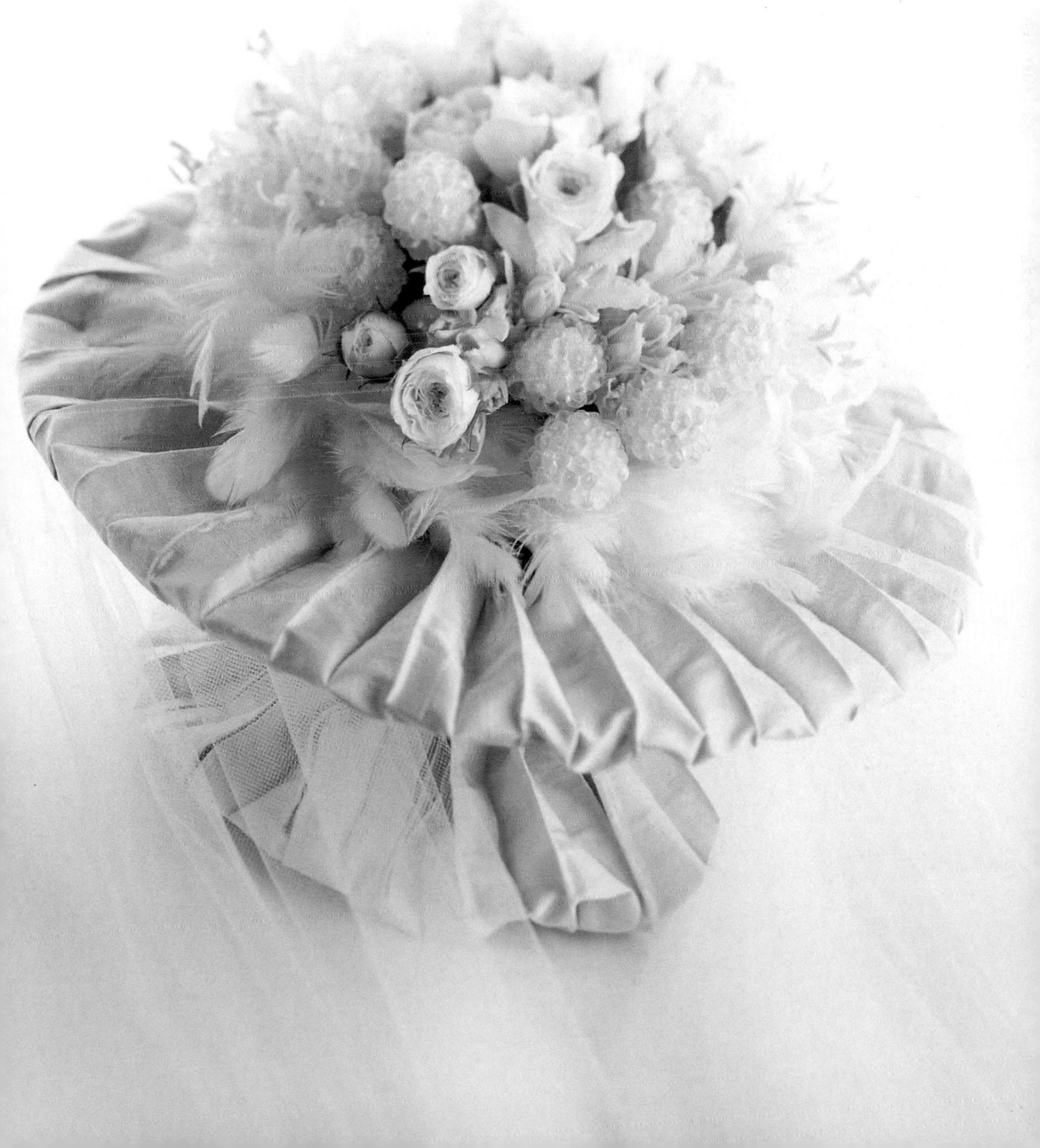

swirling Acacia

Yellow carnations are enlivened by a flower and foliage wreath.

1 With copper beading wire, assemble tufts of *Acacia* into a garland. Join the ends together to create the wreath.

2 Bend four lengths of heavy-gauge wire into hairpins. Slide them onto the vine wreath, and insert them into the sides of a saturated bouquet holder.

3 Fill the bouquet holder with carnations, forming a ball-shaped cluster.

Tufts of deliciously fragrant *Acacia*, wired into a swirling wreath formation, make an ideal spring accent for this lemony mound of yellow carnations. The spiky *Acacia* foliage, assembled to flow in one direction, adds form and movement to the otherwise static design.

Standard carnations, with their large blossoms, make filling the bouquet holder easy. However, miniature carnations could also be used with equal effectiveness. In either case, look for the most interesting varieties, including some of the newest multicolored offerings, to coordinate with the *Acacia* wreath.

materials:

Acacia
carnations
copper beading wire
heavy-gauge wire
Bouquet Mates bouquet holder

1 Form a large wreath using several strands of artificial wired vines.

Fresh and artificial wreaths form a multi-layer composition.

A collection of three wreaths, including a handcrafted artificial vine wreath and two creatively enhanced *Casuarina* wreaths, beautifully showcase a summery arrangement of Oriental lilies, *Gerberas* (with their petals removed), and larkspur. The wreaths, each formed in different sizes and laid atop one another, give the creation a dimensional, multilayer appearance.

Decorative coverings for the *Casuarina* wreaths—pink organza ribbon on one and copper and silver beading wire on the other—add unexpected textures and soften the transition from the florals to the rough-hewn artificial vine wreath.

2 Slide hairpins, made from heavy-gauge wire, onto the vine wreath, and insert them into a saturated bouquet holder. Disguise each of the hairpins with a wrapping of wired vines. Arrange the florals.

3 Form two *Casuarina* wreaths. Wrap one with organza ribbon, and wrap the other with silver and copper beading wire. Add them to the bouquet, securing them in the foam with hairpin-shaped wires.

materials:

'Le Reve' lilies
Gerberas
larkspur
Casuarina
artificial wired vines
heavy-gauge wire
organza ribbon
beading wire
Bouquet Mates bouquet holder

99 berry wrap

1 String *Hypericum* berries onto beading wire to form a berry garland. Coil the garland around the PVC wreath.

2 Bend four lengths of heavy-gauge wire into hairpins. Slide them onto the berried wreath, and insert them into a saturated bouquet holder.

3 Arrange the chrysanthemums in the bouquet holder. Disassemble a vine wreath, and use some of the vines to form a smaller wreath. Bind the vines with beading wire. Secure the wreath in the bouquet with hairpin-shaped wires.

Two textural wreaths enable these chrysanthemums to shine.

A garland of *Hypericum* berries, coiled around a basic PVC wreath, is the foundation of this glorious autumnal composition. The berry-wrapped wreath, as well as a second wreath of wire-enhanced vines, encircles a sumptuous mound of fall-hued chrysanthemums.

Gorgeous enough to be used alone, the chrysanthemums require no ornamentation, but amid their wreath trappings, both of which lend wonderful texture and color to the design, the blossoms truly shine. Chrysanthemums are available in a fabulous assortment of colors and forms, many of which would coordinate beautifully with the wreath enhancements.

materials:

chrysanthemums
Hypericum berries
beading wire
heavy-gauge wire
PVC wreath
vine wreath
Bouquet Mates bouquet holder

100 heather ring

An easy-to-make wreath accessorizes a profusion of flowers.

1 With copper beading wire, bind two stems of heather together. Continue adding heather, binding each piece to the others with the wire, until a wreath is formed.

2 Bend four lengths of heavy-gauge wire into hairpins. Slide them onto the heather wreath, and insert them into the sides of a saturated bouquet holder.

3 Arrange the *Alstroemeria*, in a rounded formation, in the bouquet holder. Coil a rosemary garland around the perimeter of the *Alstroemeria* blossoms.

A lavish cluster of white *Alstroemeria* is encircled by a profusion of tiny pink heather blossoms which have been formed into a small wreath. Attached to the bouquet holder with hairpin-shaped wires, the heather wreath beautifully accessorizes the profusion of white blossoms.

Fragrant rosemary, bound into a rope-like garland, is coiled atop the heather wreath, adding a seasonal element and complementing the pink-hued heather. Finishing the design in style, two wide streamers, made from dovetail-cut satin ribbon, are attached to wired picks and inserted into the arrangement.

materials:

Alstroemeria
heather (*Erica persoluta*)
rosemary
copper beading wire
heavy-gauge wire
satin ribbon
wired picks
Bouquet Mates bouquet holder

A versatile bouquet suitable for events throughout the year.

Composed of lilies, roses, kangaroo paws, hanging *Amaranthus*, and more, this elegant bouquet, in both its color and texture, is suitable for any season. The premium blooms, as well as the loose crescent shape defined by the cascading fern, suggest formal applications.

Two creative ribbon-and-ivy treatments offer unexpected elements. For example, sparsely foliated ivy vines are braided with wide chiffon ribbon to form the two loops, which add dimension. And placed in the heart of the bouquet are small rose-like buds that are made by wrapping knotted chiffon ribbon with short strands of the partially stripped ivy.

1 Randomly remove leaves from several ivy vines until only a few leaves remain on each vine.

2 Braid two of the partially stripped ivy vines with a length of wide chiffon ribbon. Insert the ivy stem into the bouquet holder.

3 Tie a knot in a short stand of chiffon ribbon. Continue tying knots until a small ball—about a half-inch in diameter—is formed. Wrap with bits of partially stripped ivy. Add a chenille stem and insert the vine-wrapped bud into the bouquet.

materials:
'Lamancha' lilies
roses
kangaroo paw
hanging *Amaranthus*
wedding fern (*Asparagus plumosus*)
diosma
Fatsia japonica
ivy vines
chiffon ribbon
Bouquet Mates bouquet holder

Florists' Review magazine is the No. 1 trade journal for professional florists. In addition to serving the needs of florists through its monthly publication, the magazine has an active book division that supplies educational products to all those with an interest in floral design. For more information, visit *Florists' Review*'s Web site at www.floristsreview.com.

All flowers pictured in this book were provided by the California Cut Flower Commission (CCFC). CCFC is a nonprofit organization representing California's flower growers. For more information, visit the CCFC Web site at www.ccfc.org.